W9-AEX-396

DATE DUE			

GREENE & GREENE

GREENE & GREENE

Furniture and Related Designs

RANDELL L. MAKINSON

with new photographs by Marvin Rand
including eight pages of color photographs

Gibbs M. Smith, Inc.
Peregrine Smith Books
Salt Lake City

To Marvin Rand

Copyright © 1979 by Peregrine Smith, Inc.

Library of Congress Cataloging in Publication Data   (Revised)
Makinson, Randell L   1932-
      Greene & Greene.
      Includes bibliographies and indexes.
      CONTENTS: Architecture as a fine art.   2.   Furniture
and related designs.
      1.   Greene & Greene.   2.   Architecture—California.
3.   Architecture, Modern—20th century—California.
NA737.G73M33   728.3   76-57792
ISBN 0-87905-023-3 (v. 1)

ISBN 0-87905-126-4 (v.1)
ISBN 0-87905-125-6 (v.2)

New photo-documentation for this book was carried out
under a grant from the National Endowment for the Humanities
in Washington, D. C., a Federal Agency. Opinions in the
text are the author's and do not necessarily represent the view
of the Endowment.

Contents

Preface

This book is written as a companion volume to *Greene and Greene—Architecture as a Fine Art* and deals with the furniture and related designs of both the firm and of Charles Sumner Greene and Henry Mather Greene independently. As the research progressed over the years it became more and more clear that the quantity of the furniture and related designs was so great that it could not be dealt with properly if included with the discussion of the development of the Greenes' architecture. Furthermore, the furniture and related designs of Greene and Greene are an art form in themselves and require the focus which separate attention places upon the subject. The extraordinary quality of design and craftsmanship, the changing character of the work, and the great variety of subjects designed by the brothers is dealt with chronologically and reviews the flexibility and speed of the brothers' quest for designs which to them appropriately paralleled the developments within their architectural work.

The phrase, Greene and Greene furniture, has been used too broadly over the years to identify the work for which they are best known. However, that era of the Greenes' designs was preceded and followed with equally significant works representative of the evolution of their talents, opportunities, and their joint and independent philosophies. Closely related are the abilities of those master craftsmen who virtually became a part of the Greene and Greene family—artisans whose individual talents coupled with their respect and devotion for the brothers transformed their two-dimensional dreams into reality.

The separate chapters of the book are so organized to focus upon the influences on the brothers and their early furniture designs, the short period of exploration and developments leading to their very personal design vocabulary, the opportunities which made possible the full unfolding of that unique style, the later period of changing client tastes, and finally the later works of each of the brothers as independent creative artists.

Over the years little has been written or published on the furnishings of the Greenes, inasmuch as most of the work has remained in private ownership and not available for public viewing. The single ongoing opportunity for public awareness of the Greenes' furnishings is the David B. Gamble house built in 1908 and bequeathed in 1966 to the City of Pasadena in a joint agreement with the University of Southern California. Since that time the opportunity for public visitation to the Gamble house has furthered the singular identification of Greene and Greene furniture with simple elegant forms, exquisite craftsmanship and finish, and the rhythmic patterns of square ebony pegs in the expressed joinery detailing. Not until the major exhibition "Greene and Greene: The Architecture and Related Designs of Charles Sumner Greene and Henry Mather Greene: 1894-1934" held at the Los Angeles Municipal Art Gallery in 1977, organized jointly by the Los Angeles Municipal Art Gallery and the University of Southern California, was there an opportunity to see the vast amount of interior work by the Greenes. Prior to that time the treatment of Greene and Greene furnishings and designs has had only the scant attention of a few short articles and the master's thesis by furniture designer John Caldwell. Following the exhibition there has been growing interest in this specialized area of the Greenes' creative talents with a technical article presently in process by Alan Marks for *Fine Woodworking* magazine featuring the systematized vernacular of the Greenes' furniture designs as a first truly American furniture expression.

The research for this study has come primarily from documents in the Greene and Greene Library, The Gamble House; the Documents Collection, College of Environmental Design, University of California at Berkeley; Avery Architectural Library, Columbia University; from members of the Greene and Hall families, the present owners of the furnishings studied; and from the enriching experience of exploring the work itself.

There are many to whom I am indebted for their genuine assistance in the research and preparation of this study and their names are listed in the acknowledgements in the rear of this volume.

I am indebted most deeply to Marvin Rand whose photographic genius has documented this study since 1958 and whose patience, genuine interest, valuable analytical comment and personal generosity have been of major importance in the production of this book; to Professor Emmet L. Wemple whose continuing council since the beginning has been invaluable to me and to the subject; to his and David Tilton's creative designs of the Greene and Greene exhibition and catalogue; to Virginia Ernst Kazor and Doris Gertmenian all of whom comprised the team which produced the exhibition; and to the National Endowment for the Arts which joined with the Los Angeles Municipal Arts Department and the School of Architecture and Fine Arts, University of Southern California who provided special funding for the exhibition.

Portions of this research have been carried out under grants from the American Institute of Architects whose Rehmann Fellowship in 1956 allowed for the early study and the National Endowment for the Humanities whose grant allowed for the photo-documentation of Greene and Greene furniture and related designs, a project carried out in association with Marvin Rand under the auspices of the School of Architecture and Fine Arts, University of Southern California.

Special appreciation for coordinated early research and assistance goes to Professors Robert Judson Clark and Robert W. Winter, Esther McCoy and Reynor Banham; to Margaret Nixon for her invaluable editing of the manuscript; Richard Firmage for his coordination of the production of the book, and to publishers Gibbs and Catherine Smith.

This portion of my overall research on Greene and Greene has been associated with my work as Curator of The Gamble House, University of Southern California. In this association special appreciation is expressed to Zohrab Kaprielian, Executive Vice President, Dr. Paul Hadley, Vice President Academic Affairs, University of Southern California; former Deans, Ralph Knowles and A. Quincy Jones, of the School of Architecture and Fine Arts; to Virginia Bissinger, Dr. Clark McCartney, Helen Carrier and the members of the Docent Council of The Gamble House.

In addition, for their invaluable assistance in obtaining

drawings and archive photographs, Dr. Adolf Placzek, Carol Falcione, Professors Kenneth Cardwell, Stephen Tobriner, and to Diane Favro, John Graves, Jay Cantor, L. Morgan Yost, LuVerne LaMotte, Edna Dunn, Mr. and Mrs. R. Donald Hall, Robert Hall, Gregson and Chad Hall, and Edward Bosley III.

Very special appreciation to those who made possible the study of the furniture, those kind owners who opened their households for study and photography; the members of the Greene families whose assistance was essential— Isabelle and Alan McElwain, Sumner and Harriott Greene, Ruth and the late Henry Dart Greene; Nathaniel and Genevieve Greene, Gordon and Betty Greene, and Bettie Greene.

For varying and special reasons James N. Gamble and the heirs of Cecil and Louise Gamble for the sharing of the Gamble family home with us all; to Irene Wright, Winifred Staniford, and the invaluable support of my secretary Jane Unruh whose understanding and added assistance has made this publication possible; to my father, Ronald R. Chitwood, and Paula and Harold Stewart whose encouragement has been essential; and finally very personal thanks to Emmet L. Wemple and David L. Tilton for their careful attention to the design of this book.

Randell L. Makinson
Pasadena

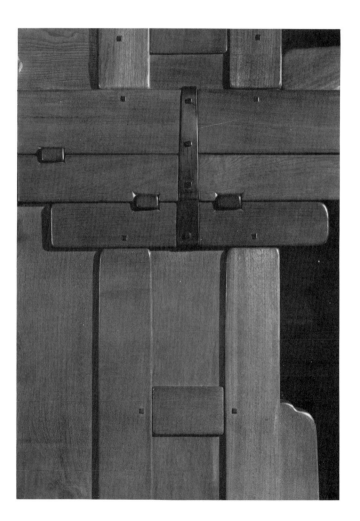

I

Influences and First Furniture Designs   1900-1904

Architects have always designed buildings, but before the latter half of the nineteenth century they had seldom so consciously and effectively related the scale of structure and the furniture to be placed within. The vigor and spirit of William Morris' philosophy and the developing Arts and Crafts Movement attracted vast numbers of individuals who had not previously been identified with the design of utilitarian objects. Homeowners and housewives were creating everything from stitchery to hammered copper pots. The times also witnessed the emergence of the architect as the designer and oftentimes maker of furniture. The Arts and Crafts Movement and the later Art Nouveau era emphasized the concepts of the artist's involvement with the full spectrum of design, be it interiors, furniture, carpets, everyday household items, or the visual and graphic arts. As a result, the fresh designs and superb craftsmanship based on Arts and Crafts principles — that design stemmed from function and form from the materials and tools used—effected the transition from the eclectic trappings of the Victorian era to the more homogeneous designs of the modern movement.

Among the Arts and Crafts Movement practitioners there were few as thoroughly and naturally devoted to its principles as California architects Greene and Greene. If composition and craftsmanship determine quality, then the Greenes were unsurpassed.

Although the major portion of the furniture and related designs were produced by the firm of Greene and Greene, Architects, these were primarily the expression of Charles Sumner Greene's creative imagination, encouraged by the support of his brother, Henry Mather Greene, and their close association with master craftsmen Peter and John Hall.

The Greenes achieved international recognition for their architectural vocabulary.[1] But the scope of their non-structural design has been largely overlooked. Even the phrase "Greene and Greene furniture" refers primarily to the furniture designed for their major residences—the ultimate bungalows — between 1907 and 1909, as these were the pieces which aroused the interest of photographers and writers. However, the Greenes' furniture and related designs spanned the period from 1900 to the mid-1930s and demonstrated their adaptability to change and the continuing development of their own philosophies and designs.

The first piece of furniture made by Charles Greene was a very simple dining table designed for his fiancée in 1900. The 48" square top was composed of geometric inlay patterns of scrap fruit woods, and cantilevered from a single straight square pedestal which flared at the base to give greater stability, and was attached with bolts and wing nuts to allow for easy and compact portability. This "wedding table" was significant not only for its direct design but also because it established Charles' early interest in the design and making of furnishings.

In the mid–1880s Charles had studied woodworking at the Manual Training High School in St. Louis. By the 1890s the Arts and Crafts Movement was in full swing. Yet this first piece of furniture did not appear until six years after the firm of Greene and Greene, Architects, had been established. Charles' delay in designing furnishings probably stemmed from the variety of his own interests; in letters to friends in Boston he often lamented the time taken up by the firm's practice which kept him from his pursuit of

1. In 1952 the brothers were presented with the coveted Citation from the national organization of The American Institute of Architects, at which time they were hailed as "Formulators of a New and Native Architecture."

Charles Sumner Greene, circa 1906.
Photograph courtesy of Los Angeles Public Library.

Henry Mather Greene, circa 1906.
Photograph courtesy of Los Angeles Public Library.

philosophy in America but also producing furniture of the highest quality and workmanship. Of his new association Stickley wrote:

> The United Crafts endeavor to promote and to extend the principles established by [William] Morris, in both the artistic and socialistic sense... Present tendencies are toward a simplicity unknown in the past.... The form of any object is made to express the structural idea directly, frankly, often almost with baldness.[4]

4. Excerpts from *The Craftsman,* Volume 1, no. 1, October 1901, pages i, 47.

Design by the Vienese architect, Josef Hoffmann, c. 1900.

Following several of his contemporaries at the turn of the century, Josef Hoffmann embraced the concept of total relation of his architecture and furnishings. Like those of Charles Rennie Mackintosh, the linearity and geometric repetition in his designs were a dramatic contrast with the more sinuous forms of the Art Nouveau movement.

Illustration of Gustav Stickley's furniture from the first issue of his magazine *The Craftsman.*

The Greenes' chair design for the Jennie A. Reeve dining room and the desk for Adalaide Tichenor, both in 1904, show clearly the influence which the first issues of *The Craftsman* had upon their own designs.

Meanwh
1902 was e
Magazine. I
many of the
indicate his
furnishings.
Between
of articles o
appeared in
the ideals o
like the Gre
Nouveau, a
stylistic dec
the straight
than the mo
pean Art N
touched a n
from his ser
scrapbook.
Nouveau ch
combined w
related to th
As the G
Crafts Move
ning in *The (*
of the inter
nishings. W
between the
seem to ha
interior desi
Of partic
room utilizir
surface deta
graphic than
But the Gre
sional and a

Within a few months the Greenes furnished much of the James Culbertson house in Stickley's furniture, selecting the very pieces that had appeared in the first two issues of *The Craftsman.*

Stickley's influence upon the Greenes went far beyond the mere use of his "United Crafts" furniture, and can be clearly seen in the interiors and furniture designs of the Greenes' work between 1902 and 1904.[5]

View of living room, James A. Culbertson house, 1902. Photograph courtesy of Mrs. Edna Dunn.

Charles Greene's early interest in Oriental timber structure as expressed in the corbels of the bay window and in the ceiling detail is blended with the rigid linearity of Henry Greene's clear leaded glass window designs and Stickley's craftsman furniture.

5. Gustav Stickley later dropped the term "United Crafts" in deference to the identification "Craftsman" furniture with notice to his
readers to look for his name associated—a reference to copies of
his work by others including his own family.

Wall lighting fixture, Josephine van Rossem
house No. 1, Pasadena, 1903.
Marvin Rand photograph.

LIVING ROOM.

Interior sketch, Mary R. Darling house, Claremont,
California, 1903.
Academy Architecture, 1903.

Charles' sketch for *Academy Architecture* magazine reveals
clearly the influence which *The Craftsman* magazine had upon
his own interior design concepts in 1903.

Next door, in the upstairs bedrooms of the Josephine van Rossem house, the first lighting fixtures designed by the firm featured several wall sconces of redwood blocks which were detailed into the board and batt paneling. Though extremely basic, these wall brackets were the beginnings of a succession of varied lighting refinements over the years incorporating leaded glass lanterns, tiffany glass, favrile shades, and occasionally lighting shielded with a folded fabric of silk pongee.

Charles' interior sketches for the Mary R. Darling house published in *Academy Architecture*, 1903, II, reveal not only his desire to control the design of the whole interior and its furnishings, but also the influence which *The Craftsman* had upon him at the time. The furniture designs and his drawings for lamps, carpets, andirons, etc. all follow the pattern of those either designed by Stickley or recommended and advertised in *The Craftsman* as appropriate for bungalow living. And, like the drawings of Hoffmann and Ellis, Charles' sketches covered every aspect of the interior, the built-in cabinetry, shelving, window seats, fabric designs, and picture frames, all harmonizing with the overall architectural statement of the space.

Little if any of the furniture in the sketches for the Darling house was built, but the Greenes were already committed to the idea of including every facet of furnishings in the design of interiors.

Early the following year, this commitment was demonstrated in the house for Jennie A. Reeve in Long Beach, California. The Greenes designed the furniture, built-in cabinetry, lighting, leaded stained glass and the detail in the wet plaster of the friezes as well as the outside lighting, fencing and landscaping—all of which related to the architectural character of the structure.

The first photographs illustrating the Greenes' full control of interiors were of the Reeve house. The dining room photographs reveal the speed with which they combined their personal artistic talent with their newly acquired craftsman attitudes to produce a completed space, highly organized and dominated by their own innovations. The influence of Stickley remained, but already there were distinct differences.

Dining room, Jennie A. Reeve house,
Long Beach, California, 1904.
Photograph courtesy Documents Collection,
College of Environmental Design, U.C.B.

In 1904 Stickley's influence is dramatic in the
chair and dining table, but Charles' imagination
and creative flair are revealed in the combined gas
and electric wall lighting fixture, and in the design
of the ceiling lantern and leaded glass. His playful
watercolor details in the plaster frieze reveal the
relaxed confidence which he had so quickly
developed.

Living room inglenook, Jennie A. Reeve house,
1904. Photograph courtesy Documents Collection,
College of Environmental Design, U.C.B.

The Greenes' interior art flourished so rapidly
that the quality of cabinetwork detailing, craftsmanship and leaded glass work usually identified
with the major houses of later years was in fact
being practiced in 1904 as evidenced by the curio
cabinet of the living room inglenook.

The versatility of Charles Greene's furniture and interior designs and his ability not only to adapt to change but, more importantly, to seek out and create change was dramatically illustrated in his work for Adelaide Tichenor, whose home was also built in Long Beach shortly after the Reeve house in 1904.

The Tichenor furniture marked a distinct change of direction, an end to the first era in the Greenes' furniture designs, and a real break with the influence of Gustav Stickley. Nearly the entire furnishings of the household were his to create or select. This was not an easy task. Charles believed in the value of inspired client participation and once wrote that "the intelligence of the owner as well as the ability of the architect and skill of the contractor limit the perfection of the result."[7] But Mrs.Tichenor challenged him constantly, as their correspondence shows, and forced him to stretch his creative imagination and talents to the fullest.

The Tichenor furniture was closely related to earlier designs. The crisp directness of form and the lack of applied decoration remains. The bold expression of the joinery was almost raw. What did change were the materials, design and spirit. Ash was the primary wood with oak used only for the doweling. Soft stains which disappeared when oiled were washed into the grains, leaving a very subtle tone to the coloration in the grain of the wood.

7. *Ibid.*

Bedroom bureau, Adelaide Tichenor house, Long Beach, California, 1904. Marvin Rand photograph.

In a refinement on the earlier design for the Reeve bureau, Charles made use of his interest in the Orient by incorporating the "lift" or abstract cloud forms in his design of the Tichenor bureau to soften the otherwise straight lines, thus giving a more graceful appearance.

What wrenched Charles from his earlier precedents and established a recognizable Greene and Greene style was his effort to blend subtly curved forms into an otherwise linear composition and, by combining an honest use of joinery giving interest and variation, arriving at a less harsh overall effect. He accomplished this with such finesse that there was no need for applied decoration.

The softened lines of these designs were derived from an interest in Oriental culture shared by both Charles and Mrs. Tichenor. For the first time he incorporated the "lift" into the movement of line—a form long used by the Oriental craftsman as an abstraction of the cloud form. In Charles' work the lift acknowledged his respect for the Oriental arts but at the same time incorporated the freshness which sprang from the spirit of personal expression in Southern California.

Over the years, a wide range of curvilinear forms became one of the major characteristics of the Greenes' architecture, furniture and leaded glass designs. The lift form as handled by both Charles and Henry Greene was distinct. The departure from the total use of the straight line removed the harsh architectural character often associated with furniture designed by architects and, instead, created pieces with a scale and appearance more humanly pleasing.

Charles' confidence in his own talents is evident in the playful way he wove decorative humor throughout the interior furnishings. Mrs. Tichenor's interest in the owl resulted in an abstracted silhouette in the design of the escutcheons for the door hardware, in the brass back panel of a bedroom washstand and in the leather panels of a large four panel screen.

In spite of the rapport and artistic respect shared by Mrs. Tichenor and the Greenes, the correspondence between them revealed very human responses to the progress of the work and the details of the designs. At times Mrs. Tichenor grew impatient. In a letter about the screen she wrote: "Can you leave your Pasadena customers long enough so that I may hope to have my house during my life time? Do you wish me to make a will telling who is to have the house if it is finished?"[8]

8. Correspondence of September 27, 1905. Courtesy Robert Judson Clark and the Documents Collection, College of Environmental Design, U.C.B.

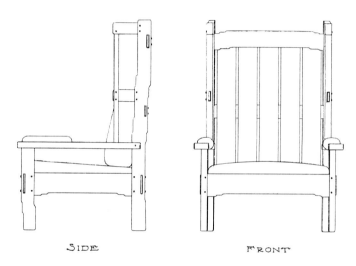

SIDE   FRONT

PLAN

BED ROOM CHAIR

TICHENOR HOUSE

Bedroom wingback chair, Adelaide Tichenor house, 1904. Drawing courtesy Documents Collection, College of Environmental Design, U.C.B.

This was the first of a series of designs for wingback chairs, each of which is handled quite differently, indicating Charles' fascination with wingback concepts.

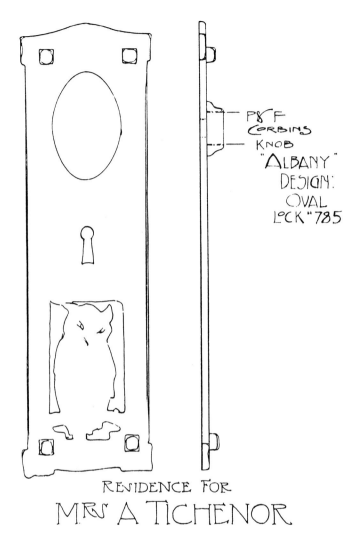

RESIDENCE FOR
MRs A TICHENOR

Escutcheon for door knob hardware, Adelaide Tichenor
house, 1904.
Drawing courtesy of Documents Collection,
College of Environmental Design, U.C.B.

The incorporation of the owl motif in the door hardware
and in other furnishings throughout the house reveals the
humor of both client and architect.

The screen is one example of Charles' imagination. Here
the mundane need for hinge hardware was handled by
Charles in such a way as to become the most dominant
feature of the entire composition, a characteristic to be
repeated throughout his career. It directly expressed its
function; yet the design went much further, combining
function and aesthetics. The hinge is dominant and in its
interlacings allowed for total flexibility in folding the parts
of the screen in any direction. The detailing was far from
being the easiest solution, but the end result suggested
simplicity.

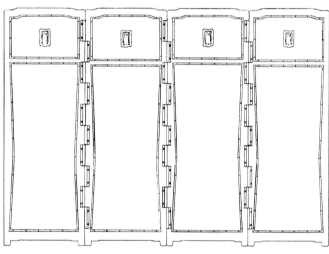

SCREEN WITH LEATHER PANELS.

Leather paneled screen, Adelaide Tichenor house, 1904.
Drawing courtesy Documents Collection,
College of Environmental Design, U.C.B.

The handling of the necessary hinging for the folding screen
so that it gives the primary character and enrichment to the
design, was a typical and sought-after characteristic of Greene
design.

The piece of furniture in the Tichenor house which best expresses the refinement in furniture design from 1904 to 1907 is a dropfront desk. The drawing itself, a beautiful graphic composition, tells the whole story. The desk is straightforward, but far removed from the Stickley linearity. Soft sculptured forms weave into the side panels and project above as bookends. Butterfly cabinet joinery, the cleted door construction, carefully organized expressed brass screw heads, and the lift of the drawer pulls complement each other in an honest but decorative manner. Here there was no need for applied decoration. Even the vertical side elements which break up the flatness of the side panels are working parts of a concealed compartment in the rear of the desk.

The boldly decorative utilization of basic structural joinery is characteristic of all of the Tichenor furniture. It is also characteristic of the Greenes' overall philosophy and speaks for the disciplined hand which Henry Greene exercised upon the later work. Charles' imagination and love for intricate detail benefitted from this restraining influence to retain the direction of the early furniture designs.

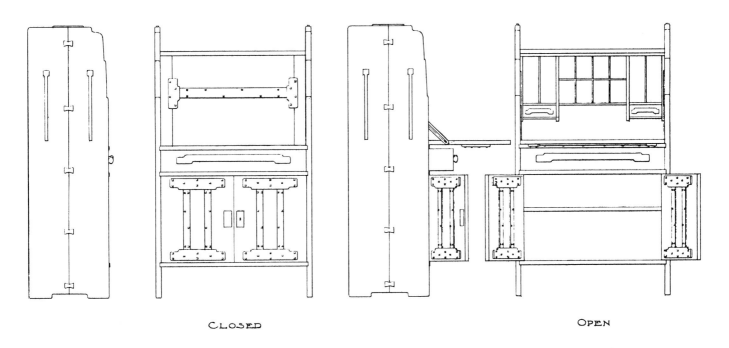

CLOSED

OPEN

DESK

Writing desk, Adelaide Tichenor house.
Drawing courtesy Documents Collection,
College of Environmental Design, U.C.B.

No ornament or furniture design better indicates the Greenes' break from the straight lines of Stickley's earlier influence. Use of curved lines, inlay joinery, and bold sculptural expression of the parts comprising the total design had now established a distinct Greene and Greene style.

Writing desk, Adelaide Tichenor house.
Marvin Rand photograph.

The Tichenor writing desk is a pivotal
 piece of furniture representative of the
first era of a distinct Greene furniture style.

Above :
Stained and leaded glass, Adelaide Tichenor house.

Right:
Wall lighting fixture, Adelaide Tichenor house.
Marvin Rand photographs.

In one year's time the development of wall sconce designs
had progressed from the brusque ruggedness of those for the
first van Rossem house (1903) to this which added the
refinements of leaded Tiffany glass and fixtures integrally
related to motifs carried out in the interior and furnishings.

In addition to the furniture, the Tichenor house exhibited
a maturing of lighting fixture designs and utilization of
stained glass leading techniques which gave Charles greater
options in his compositions. Thin sheet lead was cut out in
patterns desired and attached to the interior leaf of the lead
came between the pieces of stained glass. In so doing
Charles had full variation in the width of line and he used
this effectively to more freely express the vine patterns of
the dining room windows and the special composition of
seagulls in flight for the windows of the downstairs bedroom. Further, by carefully selecting pieces of Tiffany glass
with orange and blue combined, the silhouette of the sheet
lead overlay gave the feeling of the gulls in flight at sunset
over the ocean just outside. In composition, quality of glass,
and in the craftsmanship of fabrication, the stained glass

Copper wall clock, Adelaide
Tichenor house, 1904.
Marvin Rand photograph.

No element of the house
escaped Charles' and his
client's attention. The clock
adds further example of
the firm's concern for graphic
composition.

lanterns for the wall lighting fixtures represented a considerable refinement over those just a few months earlier for Jennie A. Reeve. Here too the "lift" softens the design which combines linear abstraction with curvilinear form within the same fixture.

One of the most unique elements within the house was a wall clock in hammered copper in which Charles worked with the forms of the numbers giving the overall design a free and playful character. Like the interiors, the Greenes fully handled the garden design and this more than the house and furnishings interpreted oriental influences more directly. Following an urgent request from Mrs. Tichenor, Charles made a special trip to the Louisiana Purchase Exposition in St. Louis to see the handling of woods which he liked very much and for the selection of interior furnishings. There his orders for the house included fabrics, pieces of Grueby pottery and some special tiles to be used in the interior detail.

Isolated examples of individual pieces of furniture carry even further the forthright structural character of Charles' work. The shelving and settle designed for the Arturo Bandini bungalow in 1903 were almost brutally straightforward. But a similar settle for Edgar W. Camp the following year shows a dramatic softening of the overall character. Here the arms were tapered and shaped to flare in response to their function and the joinery and the edges of the wood members were rolled. The lines of the bookshelving integrated into the wall paneling were likewise softened and sculpted.

In the short span of just two years, 1902–1904, the firm had entered into and become a significant part in the Arts and Crafts Movement in America. The Greenes were of course influenced by the publications of the day; but at the same time they were constantly exploring, developing, changing and refining their work and eagerly drawing from new clients the challenges which would drive them on to greater achievements.

In the two years following the Tichenor designs, the Greenes' continuing interest in Oriental art and their association with several highly gifted craftsmen would give added impetus to the variety and refinement of their furniture until they were producing art forms which established them among the foremost figures of the Arts and Crafts Movement in America.

Table lamp, Adelaide M. Tichenor house, 1904.
Courtesy of Documents Collection,
College of Environmental Design, UCB.

This lamp was the first of the few table lamps designed by the Greenes. The lamp shade depicts ocean scenes and is one of the rare designs where Greene and Greene reflect the popular forms of the Art Nouveau.

II

Developments in Design and Craftsmanship   1904-1907

In the early years Charles and Henry had considerable difficulty in finding craftsmen sufficiently skilled to meet their very high standards of workmanship. In the Pasadena area there were no cabinet shops equipped with the tools, machinery, and trained personnel to produce their custom designed furniture. It is not known where the Tichenor and other earlier pieces were actually built. In 1905, however, they became associated with the master woodscraftsmen Peter and John Hall and with the leaded glass artisan Emil Lange. It was the combined talents of these three men in collaboration with numerous other craftsmen whom the Greenes attracted which made possible the fine quality as well as the quantity of Greene and Greene furnishings during the next six years.

Peter and John Hall were born in Stockholm, Sweden—Peter in 1867 and John in 1864. By 1871 the Hall family had moved to Illinois and finally settled in Rock Falls. Neither Peter nor John had any formal training in woodworking; both were essentially self-taught craftsmen.

Peter came to Pasadena in 1886 and within a few years had won recognition as the best stair builder on the West Coast. Between 1889 and 1892 he worked in Seattle and Port Townsend, Washington. He then returned to Pasadena at the request of Charles Armstrong Roberts, a painting contractor, to do the stair and mantelwork for the large residence of Professor Thaddius Lowe. Here he met Roberts' daughter, Lida Alice, who rode down to the Lowe house every week with the payroll, and a little more than a year later they were married.

Meanwhile John Hall had followed his brother to the West Coast. His pencil sketches indicate his major role in the design and work on the woodcarving for the new courthouse in Port Townsend: the commission that had taken Peter north from Pasadena. John was a sensitive and somewhat retiring artist. In later years he preferred to work for his brother rather than to assume a leadership role. Nevertheless, his creative drive was as vigorous as that of Charles Greene and had been apparent at an early age. His first designs were dated 1880, when he was sixteen, and many of these were sketches for his carvings.

During the 1890s Peter and John Hall were employed by the Pasadena Manufacturing Company. In 1897 Peter held the position of bench hand and John that of carpenter. By 1899 John was foreman, doing additional carvings for work in Port Townsend as well as designing numerous houses on his own. In 1900 Peter was working on his own as a stairbuilder; two years later he became a building contractor.[1]

Peter Hall met Charles and Henry Greene while he was engaged in the modifications for the first Dr. William T. Bolton house which had been designed by the Greenes. The three men developed a great respect for one another as artist craftsmen, and it has been generally assumed that Charles and Henry induced Peter Hall to build and equip his own shop in order to handle the specialized work then on the Greenes' drawing boards. On June 15, 1906, within a few months of meeting the Greenes, Peter Hall took out

1. Information on Peter and John Hall has been compiled from interviews with Leonard W. Collins, senior draftsman for Greene and Greene; with Mrs. Guy E. Hodgkins, Mr. and Mrs. R. Donald Hall, Mr. and Mrs. Robert Hall, Mr. and Mrs. Gary Hall, Gregson and Chad Hall, members of Peter Hall's family; and from members of the John Hall family.

a building permit for the construction of a one-story carpentry shop for himself to be located at 900 South Raymond Ave., Pasadena. Meanwhile, his first work for the Greenes was minor alterations to the Todd Ford house. This commission was immediately followed by the contract for the construction and furnishings for one of the Greenes' most important works, the Henry M. Robinson house.

While the Greenes were demanding more and more from woodcraftsmen, they were also attempting to refine the process of leading in Charles' stained glass designs. The limitation of the uniform dimension of the leading had prompted Charles to improvise by using cut sheet lead as an overlay in order to add greater variation in line width and form. As effective as this was, it lacked refinement when related to the Greenes' woodwork. Therefore, in their search for a master glass fabricator, the Greenes approached the firm of Sturdy-Lange.

Emil Lange had come from a Milwaukee brewing family and had worked for some years in the leaded glass shop of Louis Comfort Tiffany's Studios in New York. Tiffany was at that time the leading figure in the production of quality glass and in the development of new techniques in fabrication. It was in his shop that Lange learned new techniques and developed his skills. After he came to California and went into business with Harry Sturdy, Lange was reputed to have the best supply of Tiffany irridescent glass in Los Angeles. Later he became more widely known for the leading techniques which he developed in response to Charles Greene's search for improved means to effect his glass designs.

Little is known of Sturdy and there is no indication of any personal association between him and the Greenes. But Emil Lange was to become part of the Greene "family" of master craftsmen. Like Peter Hall, Lange's first major work for Greene and Greene was for the Henry M. Robinson house.

There were numerous other master craftsmen whose combined talents and respect for Charles and Henry Greene would make possible some of the finest examples of Arts and Crafts furniture in America. Among them, however, Peter and John Hall and Emil Lange stood out as the major support in the Greenes' quest for excellence.

Peter Hall circa 1910.
Photograph courtesy of Mr. and Mrs. Robert Donald Hall

John Hall circa 1920.
Photograph courtesy of Mr. and Mrs. Robert Donald Hall.

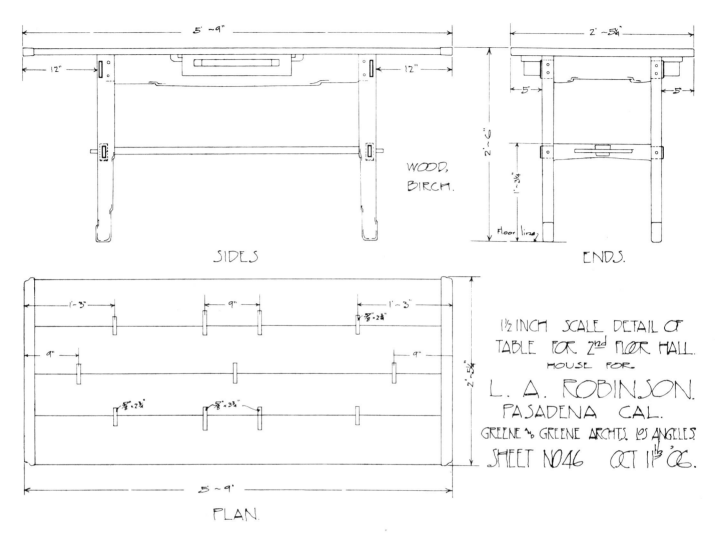

5'~9"

12"   12"

WOOD,
BIRCH.

2'~5¼"

5"   5"

2'~6"

1'~3¾"

Floor line,

SIDES   ENDS.

1'~3"   9"   1'~3"

⅝"×2¾"

9"   9"

2'~5¼"

⅝"×2¾"   ⅝"×3¾"

5'~9'

PLAN.

1½ INCH SCALE DETAIL OF
TABLE FOR 2nd FLOOR HALL.
HOUSE FOR.
L. A. ROBINSON.
PASADENA   CAL.
GREENE ⅋ GREENE ARCHTS. LOS ANGELES
SHEET NO 46   OCT 11th '06.

Drawing of table for second floor hall, Henry M. Robinson
house, Pasadena, 1906.
Drawing courtesy Avery Architectural Library.

While this and other designs for the Robinson furniture
related closely to the late period of the Greenes' early style,
the living and dining room pieces introduced new directions
and further refinements in detailing, materials and form.

Between the Tichenor house and furnishings of 1904 and the ultimate bungalows between 1907 and 1909, the most significant commission was the large home and furnishings for Henry M. Robinson begun in 1905. Here, as with their other wealthy clients, the Greenes were given ample creative opportunity, and Charles was able to continue refining his furniture and related designs. The Robinson furniture is a delicate blend of Charles' earlier ideas with the later refinements which broke completely with previous designs and set the stage for a distinct style.

Four designs in particular bear a close relationship to the furniture for Mrs. Tichenor a year earlier: a desk and library table for the den, the second-floor hall table of birch, and the entry hall seat of white cedar and oak. To some students of Greene and Greene furniture these pieces represent a closer tie to the philosophies of the Arts and Crafts Movement and are therefore held in higher regard than some of the later and more refined designs. Like the Reeve and Tichenor furniture, they possess a directness in form, joinery and materials identified with the more modest bungalow designs.

Entry hall shoe bench, 1906.
Courtesy of Documents Collection, College of Environmental Design, UCB.

Joinery of both the bench and the stairwell construction were carefully interrelated.

Library table for den, 1906.
Marvin Rand photograph.

The simple graceful lines of the den table elegantly bridge the two stylistic concepts within the Robinson furnishings.

Two important elements—materials and form—dramatically separated the living room and dining room pieces from all previous furniture by the firm. In both areas fine mahogany woods were used for the first time. Mahogany was used subsequently over a long period of time. Second, and just as important, was the carry-over from the Tichenor furniture of Charles' interest in Oriental forms. However, here he was strongly influenced by Chinese household furniture forms dating as far back as four centuries. This is particularly felt in the dining chairs and the living room couch. Moreover, Charles' fascination with Japanese temple structural joinery was demonstrated in the base of the Robinson dining table, the top of which became a form frequently used for dining tables for later clients. The Oriental influence was also suggested in the rest of the living room furniture.

Dining room armchair, 1906.
Marvin Rand photograph.

In a sudden and major departure from earlier concepts, the Robinson dining chairs took their forms almost directly from Chinese household furniture dating back as far as four centuries.

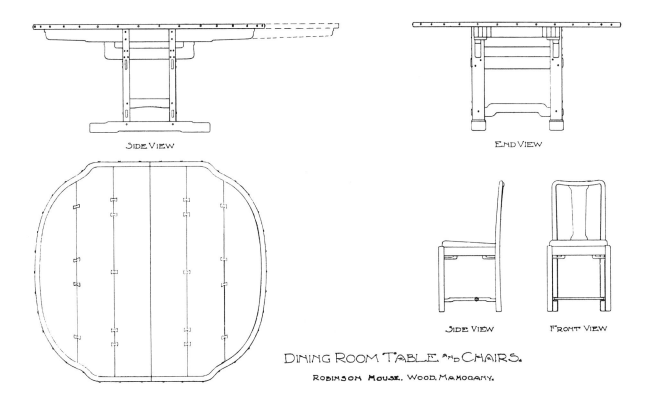

SIDE VIEW   END VIEW

SIDE VIEW   FRONT VIEW

DINING ROOM TABLE AND CHAIRS.

ROBINSON HOUSE. WOOD, MAHOGANY.

Drawing for dining table and chairs, 1906.
Drawing courtesy Documents Collection, College of Environmental Design, U.C.B.

Clean, simple lines of the table pedestal reflect the Greenes' regard for temple construction and at the same time provide for the stability necessary for extending the table to double its length without separating the supportive structure. The 'cloud lift' interpretation given to the form of the top of the table was repeated several times for other clients; however, in each instance the supporting bases were different.

Right:
Dining table, 1906.
Marvin Rand photograph.

Left:
Wall gas lighting fixture, 1906.
R. L. Makinson photograph.

Due to frequent breakdowns in power and as a carry-over of tradition gas lighting was often installed and detailed to blend with the electric lighting fixtures.

Clear leaded glass windows of upper level of entry hall, 1906. Whitland Locke photograph.

The Robinson house was also a testing ground for leaded stained glass, lighting fixtures, andirons, as well as the overall development of the house. Particularly interesting is the variation in these elements within the same structure. Some elements are far more sophisticated than others and yet all seem quite appropriate in their own places.

The den related far more to earlier and more rustic designs while the dining and living rooms reached new levels of refinement. The leaded glass compositions for the den suggest some of the glass designs of Frank Lloyd Wright which were sometimes carried out by Orlando Giannini. That Giannini might have been involved in the fabrication of the den windows of the Robinson house is not entirely out of the question for he was in Pasadena on commissions for other architects during that period. However, the glass work for the entry windows and for the major lighting fixtures has a distinctly different character and appears to have been the first work of Emil Lange for Greene and Greene.

The chandeliers and the major lighting fixtures of stained glass for the Robinson house marked a new era for the Greenes. Lighting design no longer dealt with the mere housing of the bulbs. It became a sculptured art form and had a major impact upon the character of the interior spaces. One of the most unusual features was the dining room chandelier which combined mosaic leaded irridescent glass with a highly sensitive and graceful mahogany framework. It was suspended from a more direct craftsman-era cedar ceiling plate of a fairly large size, and equipped with weights of boxes in mahogany with finger lap and ebony square peg joinery to allow the entire fixture to raise and lower by a system of suspended leather straps.[2] In the hands of one less sensitive than Charles Greene, such a complex concoction of forms and elements could have been disastrous. In his hands it became a beautiful and sensitive work of art.

2. The use of the square ebony peg identified with the Greenes' work appears first in the furniture for Dr. and Mrs. William T. Bolton and that for Mrs. Belle Barlow Bush in 1906. However, the shaping of the ebony pegs of the Robinson chandelier is representative of the refinement of 1907, suggesting that the interior furnishings for the Robinson house spread out over several years.

Den table lamp, circa 1906.
Marvin Rand photograph.

Fabric of silk pongee screens the
lighted open patterns of the red oak
shade which is supported by
metal arms joined and fastened
with specially cast triangular metal
lag screws.

Above:
View of living room looking into entry hall to the left with door to den to right, 1906.

Photograph courtesy Documents Collection, College of Environmental Design, U.C.B.

Oriental influences can be seen in the arm of the couch, the inset carvings of the bookcase and in the furnishings of the entry hall. Andirons, lighting and gas fixtures were a bold part of the enrichment of the space.

Left:
Living room desk, 1906.
Marvin Rand photograph.

Throughout the interior and exterior, the Robinson house provided the Greenes with the prospect of integrating all parts of the structure and the furnishings; and they took full advantage of this opportunity. They were so successful that other clients of substantial means were attracted to the firm.

Meanwhile clients of more modest means continued to request Charles' earlier furniture designs which were more appropriate for the smaller wooden bungalows. One of these clients was Josephine van Rossem for whom they had previously built two houses. In the third house for her—designed for her own occupancy—the furniture related more directly to the Tichenor designs, but at the same time exploited the bold expression of cleted door construction and repetitive use of exposed screws with such skill that the boldness of the design became graceful through the careful handling of scale and proportion.

Of major significance in the van Rossem design is the treatment of the paneling of the dining room. Here the Greenes used a repetitive rectangle in the detail of the vertical boarding and thus added a decorative element and a scale to the space. The repetitive geometry had a realistic three-dimensional quality consistent with the overall expression of joinery in the all wooden structure.

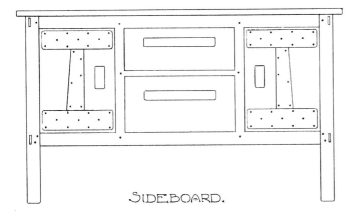

SIDEBOARD.

Dining room sideboard, Josephine van Rossem house No. 3, Pasadena, 1906.
Drawing courtesy Documents Collection, College of Environmental Design, U.C.B.

Raw screw fastenings and wooden structural cleats were treated so forcefully, yet carefully, that they gave character and individuality to this style of Greene designs.

Dining room, Josephine van Rossem house, 1906.
Photograph courtesy Mr. and Mrs. Walter J. van Rossem.

Deeply revealed detailing of the wall paneling of the van Rossem dining room is a classic example of three-dimensional character of the Greenes' geometric joinery, and has the feeling of the work of Charles Rennie Mackintosh in Queen's Cross Church, London.

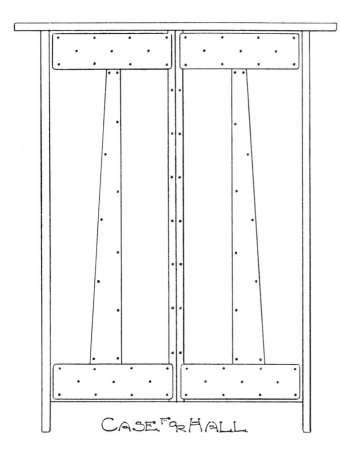

CASE for HALL

Hall case, Josephine van Rossem house, 1906.
Drawing courtesy Documents Collection,
College of Environmental Design, U.C.B.

In a similar modest manner, the sideboards for the John Bentz and Charles Willett bungalows is representative of the Greenes' ability to relate their furniture designs to other parts of their work.

During this period the Greenes extended their conception of total design to include exterior spaces as well as the interiors of their structures. They began to develop garden furniture and some elements of the streetscape. In the design for the gates of the Oaklawn subdivision, Charles had a chance to develop his interest in wrought iron, another area in which the firm developed compositions which soon became as identifiable as their architecture and furniture.

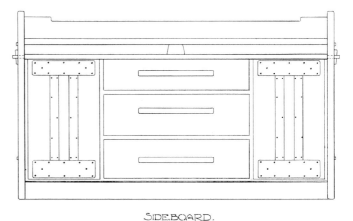

SIDEBOARD.

Sideboard, John C. Bentz house, Pasadena, 1906.
Drawing courtesy Documents Collection,
College of Environmental Design, U.C.B.

The simple and direct designs of the Bentz and Willett sideboards were typical examples of the furniture—separate or built-in—which the Greenes tastefully integrated into the design of so many of their bungalows large and small.

Wrought iron gates for Oaklawn Portals, South Pasadena Realty and Development Co., 1906.
Marvin Rand photograph.

Regardless of materials, the movement of line emanating from the hand of Charles Greene produced compositions of sculpture in the most modest of utilitarian elements.

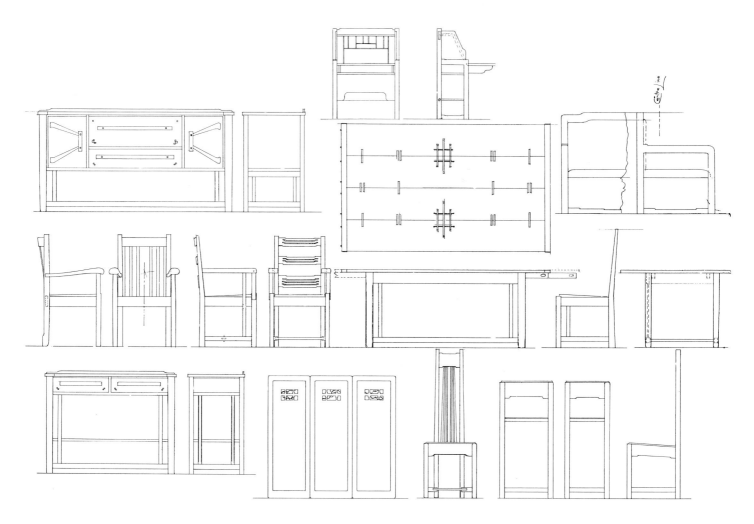

Preliminary sketches for furniture, Dr. and Mrs. William T. Bolton house, Pasadena, 1906.
Drawing courtesy Documents Collection, College of Environmental Design, U.C.B.

Dr. Bolton died unexpectedly before the house was completed. The dining room furniture was being made, completed and placed into the house. The balance of the designs as well as others were then commissioned and made for the first rental occupant of the house—Mrs. Belle Barlow Bush.

In July of 1906, shortly after work was started on the Robinson house and a month after Peter Hall took out the building permit for his carpentry shop, construction began on a second house for Dr. William T. Bolton. Both Dr. and Mrs. Bolton were enthusiastic about the Greenes' interior furnishings and consequently ordered many pieces of furniture for their living room, dining room, and entry hall. The Bolton designs demonstrated the rapid development of Charles' work with different materials, techniques, forms and detail and represented another major step toward a distinct Greene style. In some pieces the lift was again expressed, although more subtly now than in earlier years.

Bolton-Bush hall chair, 1907.
Photograph courtesy Greene and Greene Library.

Bolton dining room sideboard, 1907.
Photograph courtesy Documents Collection,
College of Environmental Design, U.C.B.

The Bolton sideboard appears to be the first fully developed use of the folded ribbon abstract inlay work which Charles later frequently utilized.

Right:
Bolton writing room desk, 1907.
Marvin Rand photograph.

In a bold effort to alleviate the usual weak support for the drop leaf desk, Charles projected the drawer and lower portion for the door to rest upon, and expressed the concept in the form of the front leg design.

Above left:
Bolton dining room chair, 1907.
Photograph courtesy Greene and Greene Library.

The less subtle handling of the lift form in the back detail is less effective in softening the strong linear quality of the back of the chair although Charles' gentle touch is clearly evident in the formation of the leg at the line of the seat.

Left:
Bolton dining room table, 1906.
Photograph courtesy Greene and Greene Library.

The carefully calculated proportioning of the secondary verticals of the leg and strut composition relate to similar details in the chairs and produce the unusual character of the Greenes' most linear dining table until Henry Greene's designs for Walter L. Richardson in 1927. Many elements of the Bolton furniture suggest that Henry may have worked closely with Charles on these designs.

Above :

Bolton dining room, 1907.
Photograph courtesy Documents Collection,
College of Environmental Design, U.C.B.

Crisp lines of the dining table and chairs are complemented
by the inlay detail of the sideboard and serving table, the
irridescent Tiffany glass patterns of the doors to the kitchen
pantry, and by the free flowing abstract paintings in the frieze.

As in the Robinson dining furniture, there was a relationship to Chinese household furniture. However, there was
a fresh and different quality about the Bolton designs in
relating the playful intensity of the folded ribbon inlay work
of the dining pieces with the severity of the repetitive vertical and horizontal structural lines. In addition, the Bolton
furniture appears to be Charles' first use of the square ebony
peg which was soon to become his trademark. But here the
ebony peg was less refined. The edges were not as sensitively rolled and the face was more flat than in latter inter-
pretations. The juxtaposition of two pegs of varying proportion touching at a corner was used only in the Bolton
furniture. Nevertheless, with the exception of the library
table, there was still a strong tie to the linear qualities in
Stickley's designs, although these were softened. In the
tables for the entry hall the Oriental influence furnished
a graceful lightness in contrast to the robust solidity of the
dining pieces.

Bush clock, 1908.
Photograph courtesy Documents
Collection, College of Environ-
mental Design, U.C.B.

Typical of several pieces designed
especially for Mrs. Bush, the clock
was adorned with inlay work of
bees which were to be symbolic of
the initials for Belle Barlow Bush.

Bush library table, 1907.
Photograph courtesy Greene and
Greene Library.

Likely the first of the Greenes' gateleg drop leaf table designs, the
library table and other designs for
Bolton and Bush furniture represent
the first use of the square ebony
peg now identified with the furniture
designs of 1907-1911.

View of Bolton-Bush writing room, circa 1908.
Drawing courtesy Documents Collection, College of Environmental Design, U.C.B.

Charles' work for Mrs. Bush included picture frames and bookplates as well as designs for curtains which were appliqued by Mrs. Bush's niece.

Bolton-Bush entry hall table, 1907. Marvin Rand photograph.

One of the most sensitive and graceful of all Greene designs, this table is strongly related, like the Robinson dining chairs, to traditional Chinese household furniture designs.

Dr. Bolton died before the house was completed and only the furniture for the dining room was finished. Mrs. Bolton moved East and rented the house, complete with the dining room furniture, to Mrs. Belle Barlow Bush. Mrs. Bush had most of the remaining furniture made. Later she had Charles design several other pieces including several small curio cabinets, a clock, small tables, and picture frames. These designs were inlaid with small bees in ebony signifying the three letters of her names: Belle Barlow Bush. Most of the furniture was produced at the Peter Hall mill, but two of the curio cabinets were made by Mrs. Bush's nephew, Walter A. Gripton, who had a cabinet shop in Pasadena. His sister, Ethel Gripton, carried out Charles' abstract patterns for applique work on the living room curtains.[3]

The curio cabinets and the clock were designed in 1908. By this time the Greenes were deeply involved in the furnishings for their ultimate bungalows and consequently these pieces reflect the increasing refinements of their most notable work.

The last piece of furniture for Mrs. Bush was a large couch for the living room. This couch is vividly remembered by the family because it took four years to complete. This delay was undoubtedly caused by the extraordinary amount of furniture being produced by this time at the Peter Hall mill for the Greenes' clients.

Mrs. Bush, like several of the Greenes' other clients, became intimately involved with and excited about Charles' interest in the total design of interiors and furnishings. Her close association with the Greenes lasted for many years. Even after she moved to Boston in 1914 she had Charles design bookplates for herself and for at least one of her daughters.

3. Correspondence with Mrs. Leet Bissell and interviews with Mrs. W. Herbert Allen, daughters of Mrs. Belle Barlow Bush.

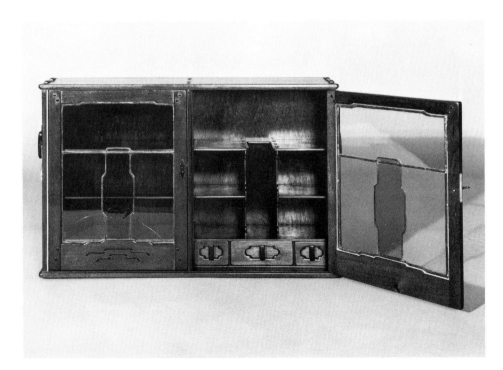

Bush curio cabinet, 1908. Marvin Rand photograph.

In August of 1908, Charles sent Mrs. Bush two designs for the small cabinet with variations of solid wood or glass doors of differing patterns. Her response called for the glass doors, and a request for special sizing of the interior shelving for a special keepsake, and left the final design completely to Charles' taste.

Far right:
Clear leaded glass window, James
A. Culbertson house alterations,
1907. Marvin Rand photograph.

The abstract flowing line work
for the stair landing windows added
to the Culbertson house are the
richest expression of Charles'
flirtation with Art Nouveau forms.

Right:
Leading detail.
Marvin Rand photograph.

During the period between 1905 and 1907, the refinements in design and in techniques of wood craftsmanship
paralleled the development in the quality of the leaded and
stained glass work. The association with Emil Lange was
reflected in some of the work for the Robinson and Bolton
houses although the glass fabrication for the John Addison
Cole house in 1907 was apparently the work of others.

Frequently the Greenes commissioned leaded stained
glass work from the Judson Art Glass Studios located on
the bluffs overlooking the Pasadena Arroyo, an area flour-
ishing with artisans.[4] On these occasions Charles or Henry
would go into the Judson Studios and work out the cartoons
for the leading design along with Judson glass artists.[5]

4. The Judson Studios joined with many of these craftsmen forming
   the Arroyo Craftsmen, an organization devoted to the Arts and
   Crafts Movement. As active as the individual artists were, the
   periodical begun by the group—*The Arroyo Craftsman*—survived
   only one issue.

5. Interviews with Horace and Walter Judson.

Major alterations and additions to the James A. Culbertson house (1902) were begun in 1906. The entry hall was enlarged, the stairwell redeveloped, the dining room totally redeveloped in the space previously housing the kitchen and a new one-story service wing added off the corner of the house.

The most significant aspects of these modifications were the refinements in the designs and craftsmanship of the interiors of the entry and dining room. Intricately patterned carvings were done for the frieze in both spaces, and de-

tailed paneling, lighting fixtures, leaded glass, ceiling relief detail, hardware, and carpet designs represented a preview of the work for the elaborate bungalows just on the horizon.

The Culbertson remodelings were the grand finale of the four year period during which the Greenes entered into the area of furniture design and evolved a style marked by originality and superb craftsmanship. Their interior work had begun with the James Culbertson house and now the period of their developmental years closed with highly significant designs for that same client.

Carved wood panels for James A. Culbertson house alterations, 1907. Marvin Rand photograph.

Charles worked daily with the woodcarvers in Peter Hall's mill. He allowed the grain of the redwood to influence his design. Water color washes were gently used on the raw wood for subtle coloration of certain details and gold leaf applied to accent running motifs.

Entry hall after remodeling, James A. Culbertson house, 1907.
Julius Shulman photograph.

With the exception of the stained glass door (the screen and
furnishings of a later generation), this photograph exhibits the
fully redesigned entry hall work of 1906 and 1907, including
the redwood frieze carvings, the subtly patterned oak wall
paneling, lighting fixtures of Tiffany leaded stained glass and
the undulating ribbon detail framing the panels of the ceiling.

III

A Distinct Style   1907-1911

By 1907 the Greenes had developed a style in both their architecture and their furniture and a confidence in themselves which attracted more and more clients. The years of experimentation were behind them. The reputation of the firm was well established. They were now able to select those clients with the vision and the means to encourage the design of interior furnishings of the highest quality in both composition and craftsmanship.

So great was the amount of work coming in that Greene and Greene were now employing up to fifteen draftsmen. Several of these, headed by Leonard W. Collins, spent most of their time on furniture drawings. Peter Hall added space and equipment to his own shops in 1907 and 1908 and placed his brother in charge of the mill and the making of furniture. This was to have a decided impact upon Charles' designs. John Hall's long experience in cabinet making clearly distinguishes the work under his supervision. Charles' pencil sketches for furniture found among John Hall's papers indicate the close professional rapport between the two men. The first conceptual freehand drawings were carefully studied by both before final detailing and construction drawings were done.

This same rapport existed between Charles and many of the master craftsmen working in the mill on furniture, carving or lighting fixtures. David Swanson—a young master craftsman from Sweden who joined Peter Hall in 1908 and later became shop foreman—vividly remembered the Greenes. Henry, he said, rarely visited the mill as he was too busy on major construction and seeing to the operation of the offices. Charles was a totally different character. He came down to the mill every morning—put on a smock and worked right with each of the workmen. He had long flowing hair and would work with the tools himself while in the shops. The men had a great deal of respect for Charles and got along with him well as long as they did not differ with him—though extremely mild and soft-spoken, he was dominating and could induce clients to spend the money required to produce such fine and intricately fabricated furniture.[1]

The mill was far better equipped than most normally identified with the hand-crafted work of the Arts and Crafts Movement. Though some of Charles' earliest and late pieces of furniture were done by him by hand, the quantity and sophistication of the furniture between 1907 and 1916 required power tools and milling capabilities which were developed in the Hall mill specifically for the Greene and Greene work. Long under-floor shafts powered by gasoline engines generated the series of belts which would come through the floor to operate the various pieces of equipment along the line. On the job sites similar small gas-engined, belt-powered equipment allowed for considerable detail and finish work.

By now Charles had developed a system of forms and joinery which allowed him complete flexibility and yet retained a genuine continuity. So basic were his concepts that his system still enables young artisan craftsmen to compose contemporary and independent designs which nevertheless relate to the spirit of Greene designs.

1. Interviews by the author with Leonard W. Collins.

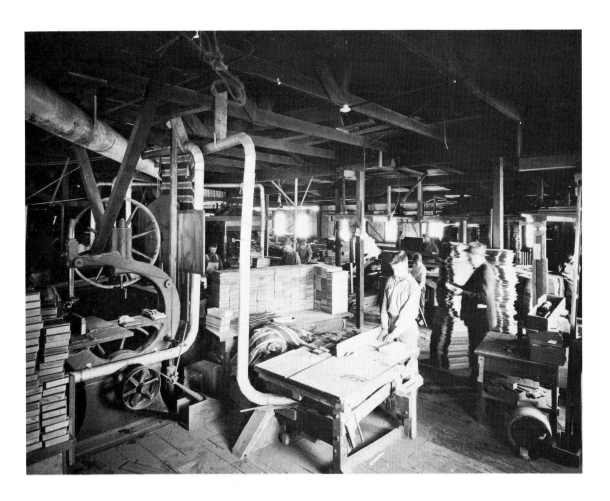

Interior of Peter Hall
Manufacturing Co.,
Pasadena, circa 1915.
Photograph courtesy Mr. and
Mrs. R. Donald Hall.

Long under-floor shafts run
by gas engines powered the belts
to operate the various pieces
of machinery.

Right:
Charles Greene preliminary
freehand sketch for Gamble
dressing table, 1908.
John Hall papers, courtesy of
Gregson Hall.

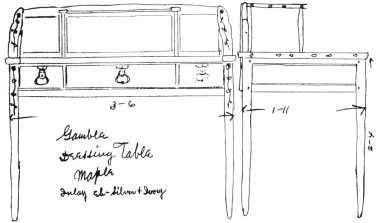

In principle, the system followed the same concepts underlying the Greenes' architecture: the total was composed of separate parts; the identity of those parts was openly expressed; the bringing together of two similar or dissimilar elements created a point of transition and the resolution of that transition often developed a totally independent third condition which both acknowledged the joining of elements and at the same time brought an enrichment to the total composition. In addition, the system of softly shaped square and rectangular ebony pegs added a playful latitude and decorative variable to the necessary task of fastening parts. In general, the ebony peg was a form of blind fastening; it covered a brass screw counter-sunk with washer into the square or rectangular hole. On occasion Charles' organization of the points of fastening were often complemented with additional pegs carrying out a rhythmic theme in the design.

Two surfaces were seldom brought together in the same

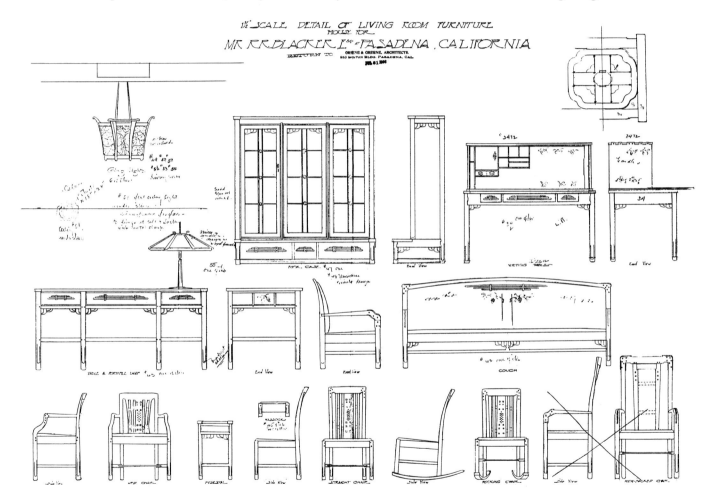

Preliminary drawing for living room furniture, Robert R. Blacker house, Pasadena, 1907.
Courtesy Greene and Greene Library.

plane. One member generally was recessed to allow the other to dominate. When necessary, as in table tops, joints were made flush with butterfly inlay joinery, and edge pieces with butt joints spliced with an edge exposed ebony spline cross-fastened by ebony pegs. Ends of wood were usually capped with a cross member and these were boldly detailed to express their attachment.

Because wood continues to expand and contract, the overall early concept was to so compose the parts of the

design that such movement could take place without apparent change in the visual character of the finished product.

Woodcraftsman Alan Marks' observations in his article for *Fine Woodworking* magazine focuses on this particular concept:

Several aspects of their table construction deserve attention. The majority of Greene tabletops and desk tops are solid wood. Others were veneered but only when the design required it, such as those with simple marquetry or inlay.

View of living room, Blacker house.
Leroy Hulbert photograph, Courtesy Greene and Greene Library.

Except for the oriental carpets and the piano the entire development of the interior was attended by the Greenes.

Detail of living room cabinet.
Marvin Rand photograph.

The corner motif was carried throughout the living room furniture. Use of the "dancing" square ebony peg joinery became the Greenes' signature throughout the years 1907-1911.

Living room cabinet, Blacker house.
Marvin Rand photograph.

Living room table, Blacker house.
Marvin Rand photograph.

Fruitwood, copper and silver inlay
of living room table.
Marvin Rand photograph.

Entry hall shoe bench with cabinet
in seat, Blacker house.
Marvin Rand photograph.

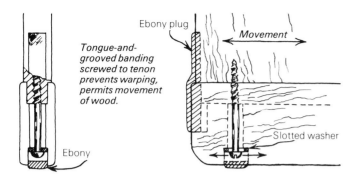

Detail of typical furniture joinery.
Drawing by Alan Marks, Courtesy *Fine Woodworking* magazine.

Detail of living room chair.
Marvin Rand photograph.

A continuous ebony spline joins the arm
and leg members and is fastened with inset
screws capped with ebony pegs. This technique was used throughout the Greenes'
furniture of the period to avoid separation
of joinery.

Others are edged with massive hexagonal or otherwise
polygonal bandings. Of the rectangular, solid wood ones,
all have banding tongue-and-grooved across the end grain
to prevent warping. They are secured with screws, not
glued. Expansion and contraction of the top is accommo-
dated in a fully satisfactory way. Bandings were drilled
with spaced, oversized holes for the screws. Rectangular
mortises were chiseled to a depth of about 3/8 in. and fitted
with slotted washers. Screws biting tightly into the tenon
secure the banding and slide back and forth in their washers
as humidity changes. The banding overlaps the tabletop
and movement of the two pieces relative to each other is
unnoticeable. Ebony plugs are glued into the tabletop, but
float in special mortises in the bandings. [2]

Joinery was accentuated. Right angle corners were frequently composed with a finger lap joint and cross pegged
with ebony. Mortise and tenon was utilized although not to
the extent found in earlier furniture. The round peg yielded
to the square. Handles were emphasized and often provided
decoration. Leather became the major material for hinging
screens and for hanging lighting fixtures. Occasionally,
when desired by clients, inlay patterns were carried out with
fruitwoods, silver, and semi-precious stones.

Although naturally there were differences between the
designs for the various clients, the similarities were more
obvious. Because of the larger budgets now available, the
woods selected and frequently used included Honduras
mahoganies of very fine grades, solid teakwood, ash, walnut, walnut, ebony, rosewood and maple. Unlike his later work,
Charles, during this period, allowed the natural grain of the
wood to provide enrichment and dealt with silhouette, form
and joinery as dominant design determinants. Soft stains
were rubbed repeatedly with boiled linseed oil and Japan
dryer until the friction produced the heat necessary for
the final finish. [3]

2. Marks, Alan. "Greene and Greene: A Study in Functional Design,"
   Fine Woodworking, (September, 1978) p. 43.

3. Interview by the author with Mr. and Mrs. R. Donald Hall.

Living room writing desk, Blacker house.
Marvin Rand photograph.

The upper writing case is detailed with leather cushions which rest on the lower table and drawer unit.

Master bedroom chiffonier, Blacker house.
Photograph courtesy L. Morgan Yost.

This unusual design has a feeling for some of the work of Charles Rennie Mackintosh in the handling of the broad brimmed cap.

Entry hall cabinet, Blacker house.
Marvin Rand photographs.

Handles for the doors emerge from the abstract
pattern of the carvings.

Wall lighting fixture for downstairs bedroom
depicts an abstract composition of clouds and
flowers and stems in the stained glass. The
fixture relates in form and joinery to the wall
and ceiling trim detail.

Entry hall "Morris chair," Blacker house.
Marvin Rand photograph.

Below:
Adjustable back hardware repeated the square peg theme in the square lag screws and positioning locks.
Marvin Rand photograph.

The first of the furnishings for the ultimate bungalow clients were those for the Robert R. Blacker house in 1907. These were followed by the David B. Gamble and Freeman A. Ford houses in 1908, for the William R. Thorsen residence in 1909, and for the Charles M. Pratt house begun in 1910. However, there was considerable overlapping, and at times work was proceeding simultaneously on these jobs.

There were thematic variations between the various projects as well as within each home. Portions of the Blacker furniture exhibit greater hints of the Orient than is felt in other works. Even the very direct simple lines of the entry hall furniture in teakwood were touched with an Oriental influence at the base of the legs. The furniture for the dining, living and master bedroom was made with Honduras mahoganies and was enriched with varying amounts of inlay work of mother-of-pearl, silver, copper and fruitwoods.

Entry hall chandeliers in teakwood and Tiffany glass suspended by leather straps, Blacker house.
Marvin Rand photograph.

Ceiling fixture of downstairs bedroom library.
Marvin Rand photograph.

Dining room chandelier,
Blacker house.
Marvin Rand photograph.

The sculptural character of the
ceiling plate and the decorative
treatment of the leather hangers
overshadow the elegant simplicity
of the stained leaded glass light
box. Slivers of irridescent glass both
reflect and emit light from the
delicate slits in the wood side
panels. A companion fixture of
square proportions hangs in the
adjoining breakfast room.

Detail of exterior entry lantern in brass and leaded stained glass with hardware for copper downspout in background. Marvin Rand photograph.

The Gamble furniture was a more straightforward statement of the Greenes' systemized vocabulary. Inlay work or carvings were featured only in the bedroom pieces and a living room writing desk, and these related directly to elements within the room. For instance, the incised design in the silver beds which Charles designed for the guest bedroom echoed the silver inlay in the wooden pieces, and the Rookwood Pottery patterns were reflected in the master bedroom furniture.

Mr. and Mrs. David Gamble also called upon Charles to design furniture for Mrs. Gamble's maiden sister, Julia Huggins, who occupied a room in the Gamble house which had been especially designed for her. The furniture for Miss Huggins again possesses that remarkable straightforward, simple character of the early Greene furniture or the best of the later designs. Gone is elaborate decoration, and the beauty of the pieces results from the grain of wood and the superb scale and proportion of the design.

Living room table, chairs, and carpet, Gamble house. Marvin Rand photograph.

The Gamble table is one of the classic designs fully featuring the various elements of the Greenes' furniture vocabulary.

View of living room featuring a portion of the fireside
inglenook, piano and carpet design, Gamble house.
Marvin Rand photograph.

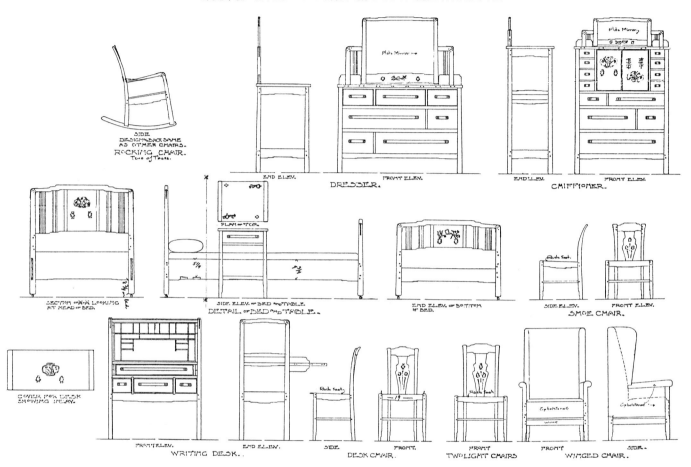

DESIGNS FOR FURNITURE FOR RESIDENCE FOR D.B.GAMBLE ESQ AT
PASADENA CALIFORNIA.
GREENE McGREENE ARCHTS 215 BOSTON BLD'G PASADENA.

Preliminary designs for master bedroom furniture, David B.
Gamble house, Pasadena, 1908.
Drawing courtesy Greene and Greene Library.

With minor detail refinements, all furniture was made with
the exception of the overstuffed winged chair.

Inlay work and proportioned drawer detail of master bedroom chiffonier, Gamble house.

Detail of inlay and joinery, master bedroom chiffonier, 1908.
Marvin Rand photographs.

Detail of carved redwood living room frieze, Gamble house. Photograph courtesy Documents Collection, College of Environmental Design, U.C.B.

Charles worked daily with the carvers evolving portions of the design from the grain of the wood. This photograph was taken following installation of the carving and prior to the placement of the lock wedges and metal strapping.

Far left:
Living room rocker.

Left:
Living room armchair, Gamble house.
Marvin Rand photographs.

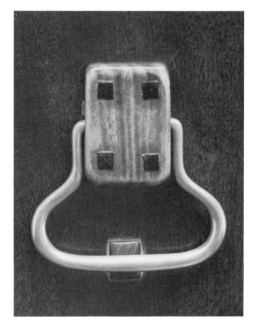

Detail of letter cabinet.
Photograph courtesy Documents Collection,
College of Environmental Design, U.C.B.

The Gamble family crest was incorporated
into the carved front panel. Side door
handles are part of the protruding tree trunk
of the wood inlay work. Details are carried
out in ebony and silver.

Above:
Living room writing desk, letter
case and lamp frame.
Photograph courtesy Documents
Collection, College of
Environmental Design, U.C.B.

Gamble guest bedroom letter
case detail.
Marvin Rand photograph.

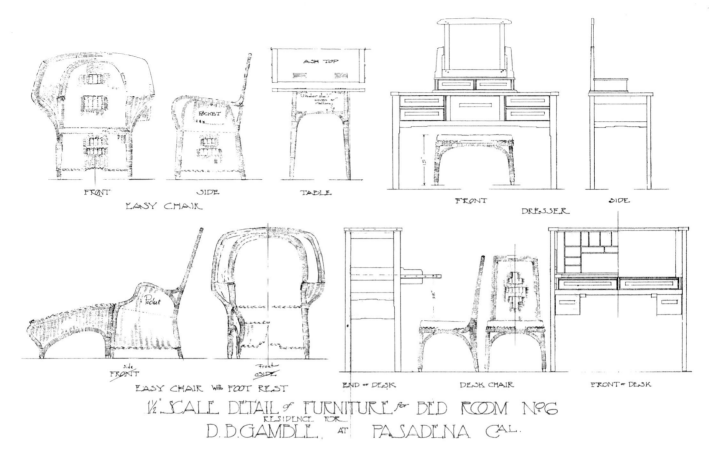

FRONT   SIDE   TABLE

EASY CHAIR

FRONT

DRESSER

SIDE

side
FRONT

Front
SIDE

EASY CHAIR with FOOT REST

END of DESK

DESK CHAIR

FRONT of DESK

1½" SCALE DETAIL of FURNITURE for BED ROOM Nº6
RESIDENCE FOR
D.B.GAMBLE, AT PASADENA CAL.

Designs for furniture for bedroom occupied by Mrs. Gamble's sister, Julia Huggins.
Drawing courtesy Documents Collection,
College of Environmental Design, U.C.B.

Charles' rattan furniture designs were rare and here were gracefully related to the wooden furniture of ash by combining the ash top table on a support of rattan and utilizing a rattan stool and chair for the dresser and desk. The stain coloring the rattan was also rubbed into the soft woods of the ash pieces, thus adding to the subtle harmony of the overall combinations.

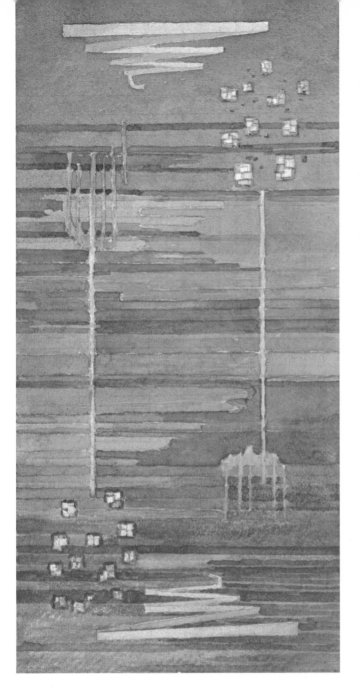

Bedroom window, Adelaide M. Tichenor house, 1904.

Living room carpet watercolor, David B. Gamble, 1908.
Courtesy of Documents Collection,
College of Environmental Design, UCB.

Right:
Entry door, Freeman A. Ford house, 1907.
Marvin Rand photographs.

Living room arm chair,
Robert R. Blacker house,
1907.

Exterior lantern, Robert R. Blacker house, 1907.

Right:
Bathroom window, Robert R. Blacker house, 1907.
Marvin Rand photographs.

Interior window, David B. Gamble house, 1908.

Guest bedroom sconce, David B. Gamble house, 1908.

Facing page:
Entry hall, David B. Gamble house, 1908.
Marvin Rand photographs.

Above:
Game room armchair, Mortimer Fleishhacker house, 1923.

Above right:
Bathroom window, Freeman A. Ford house, 1907.

Right:
Dining room china case doors, Thomas Gould Jr. house, 1924.

Facing page:
Living room detail, William R. Thorsen house, 1909.
Marvin Rand photographs.

Interior wall lanterns, James Culbertson house, 1907.
Marvin Rand photograph.

View of living room of the Freeman A. Ford house looking into entry hall. Photograph: *Architectural Record*, December, 1913.

Following several variations with winged chairs for previous clients, the Ford chair is the classic. It was a direct and natural product of the articulated system of furniture construction that had emerged by 1908. In spite of its apparent massive scale and rigid geometry it blended well with the lighter pieces of furniture in the large and boldly detailed living room.

One of Charles' most unusual designs was the wingback chair for the Freeman A. Fords in 1908. Previously he had experimented with wingback chairs for Mrs. Tichenor in 1904, for Mrs. Bush in 1906 and for the Gamble bedroom in 1908—the latter a fully overstuffed version. But for Freeman A. Ford, the wingback chair was developed primarily in wood in a linear and planar composition. Instead of appearing clumsy, this chair had both charm and distinction and at the same time blended easily into the lighter furnishings of the living room. The rest of the furniture was equally charming and revealed Charles' romance with form. In the backs of the dining chairs the splats have a feeling for American Indian design, and the ebony pegs are more irregularly shaped and canted as if to prove that absolute order was something to be defied.

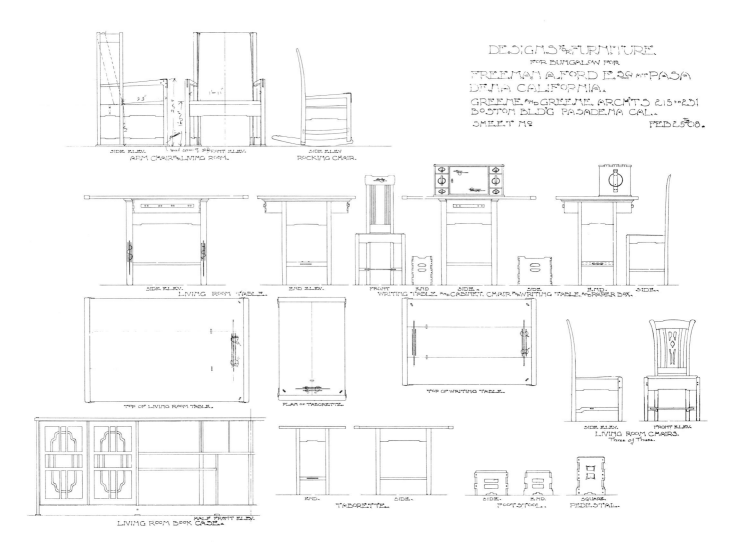

Preliminary designs for living room furniture for the Freeman
A. Ford house, Pasadena, 1908.
Drawing courtesy Greene and Greene Library.

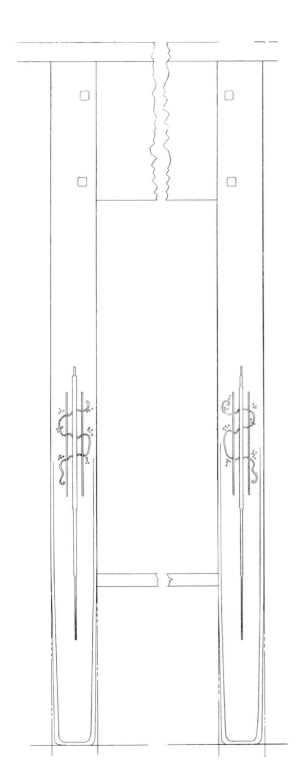

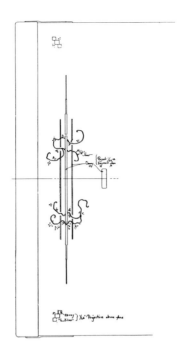

Detail of inlay of fruitwood, ebony and silver for taborette, Ford house. Drawing courtesy Documents Collection, College of Environmental Design, U.C.B.

Letter case for living room table, Ford house.
Photograph courtesy Greene and Greene Library.

Nearly the whole of the Greenes' detail system is expressed in this piece: the finger lap joint, square ebony peg, variations of handle treatment, silver piano hinging, ebony key and keyhole escutcheon, abstracted cloud and vine inlay work, and the use of leather to protect the table top from scratches.

Leaded glass and joinery detail of entry to dining room door,
Ford house.
Marvin Rand photograph.

86

Dining room wall lantern.
Marvin Rand photograph.

Hall ceiling lantern in metal and irridescent glass, Ford house.
Whitland Locke photograph.

The square peg motif was translated into the head detail for lag screws and metal fasteners.

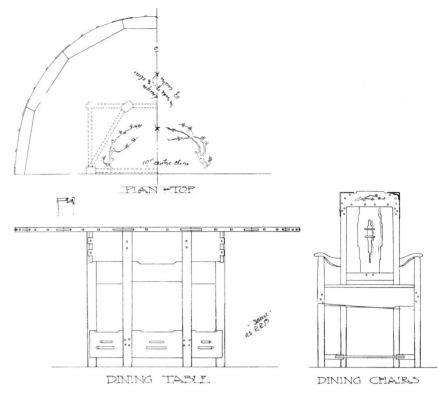

DINING TABLE

DINING CHAIRS

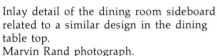

Inlay detail of the dining room sideboard related to a similar design in the dining table top.
Marvin Rand photograph.

Right:
Preliminary sketches for portion of dining room furniture, William R. Thorsen house, Berkeley, California, 1909.
Drawing courtesy Documents Collection, College of Environmental Design, U.C.B.

Peter Hall sent craftsmen from his shops in Pasadena to Berkeley where the furniture was made in the basement "Jolly Room" of the Thorsen house.

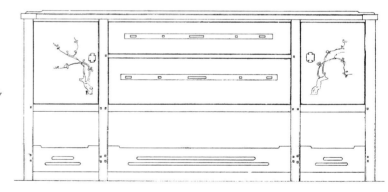

Although fewer in number, the designs for William R. Thorsen are some of the most classical and elegant of Charles' work. The sideboard and server in the dining room are masterpieces in scale and proportion. The handling of the lift in these pieces transcends the Oriental influence and becomes a new and fresh expression of Charles' artistry.

Dining room serving table.

Classic proportions and the further refinement of the oriental cloud motif give the overall design a simplicity which is as contemporary today as it was startling in 1910.

Below right:
Dining table, Thorsen house.

Below left:
View of dining host chair illustrating the unusual twist in the arm design, a concept used frequently in Greene furniture.
Marvin Rand photographs.

Above left:
Detail of dining room, Thorsen house.

The overall combination of paneling, lighting and detail of the Greene interiors were so sensitively woven together that the end result was a sculptural "symphony."

Above right:
Detail of small dining room wall case.

Charles' abstract painting of vines in the frieze is seen through the window design of clear and softly stained irridescent glass.

One design of the four intricately designed fire screens made for the Thorsen house. Marvin Rand photographs.

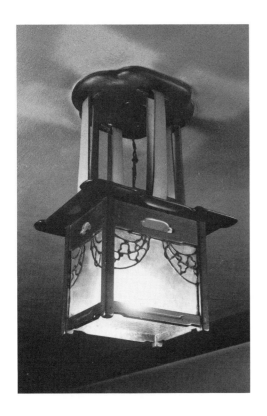

Above right:
One of two ceiling lanterns of the dining room.

Above left:
Entry hall lantern, Thorsen house.

Detail of firescreen.
Marvin Rand photographs.

The floral and folded ribbon design in the firescreen appeared repeatedly in many variations in Charles' designs after 1910.

View of living room, Thorsen house.
Marvin Rand photograph.

Wrought iron gate to side gardens, Thorsen
house.
Marvin Rand photograph.

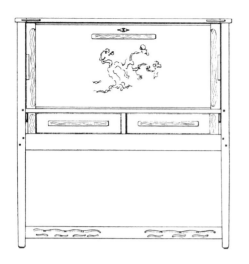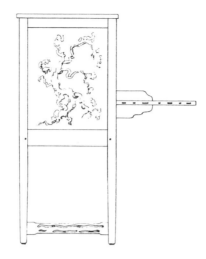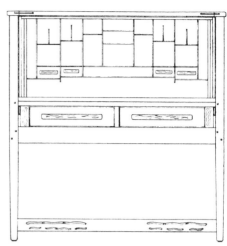

FRONT CLOSED.   SIDE.   FRONT OPEN.

DESK.

SILVER WIRE INLAY ON HANDLES.
PERFORATIONS ON LOWER RAILS.

Above:
Finished drawing for living room desk, Pratt house.
Drawing courtesy Documents Collection,
College of Environmental Design, U.C.B.

Left:
Detail of ebony key and keyhole escutcheon, silver inlay of
dropfront handle and fruitwood tree inlay of door of Pratt
living room desk.
Marvin Rand photograph.

The Charles M. Pratt furniture also had its own individual qualities. There were similar details and uses of the lift, but the heights of the ladderbacks of the chairs and rockers was unusual and pleasing. There is considerable wood inlay in the front and side panels of the desk and silver inlay in the handles of the library table. But in spite of the power and coloration of these inlays, the handling is subordinate to the overall forms and adds more of a textural effect which, in the case of the drop-front desk, compensates for its large scale.

View of end of living room, Charles M. Pratt house, Ojai, California, 1909. Marvin Rand photograph.

Above:
Clear leaded glass sliding door of living room bookcase, Pratt house. Marvin Rand photograph.

In a beautifully restrained and quiet composition, the leading design combines both the linear and sinuous line work identified with the Greenes' art.

Pratt house living room desk photographed in the Peter Hall mill. Photograph courtesy Greene and Greene Library.

Far left:
Octagonal living room table, Pratt house.

Left:
Frame of classic ladder-back rocking chair, Pratt house. Photographs courtesy Greene and Greene Library.

Detail of living room timber joinery and lantern, Pratt house.
Marvin Rand photograph.

Capitalizing on the difficult, the Greenes were at their best when confronted with the bringing together of numerous seemingly unrelated elements.

Above:
One of several living room leather armchairs, Pratt house.

Dining room chandelier
of mahogany and Tiffany
irridescent glass detailed
with bits of jade.
Marvin Rand photographs.

Applique pattern for living room curtains, Earle C. Anthony house, Los Angeles, 1909.
Drawing courtesy Documents Collection, College of Environmental Design, U.C.B.

The dining tables as well as the library tables generally exhibited both a refinement of earlier concepts as well as variations. For the Blacker house the table was stationary and made larger by the placement of a related breakfast table at the end, whereas the Gamble and Pratt tables followed the earlier form of the Robinson table and concentrated on the elaborate cantilever structure to permit the addition of leaves without the separation of the base. The base of the Gamble dining room table was so carefully proportioned, detailed and finished that it became a piece of wood sculpture. Successful as the Gamble table was, however, there was a directness in the functional bare bone structure of the Pratt and Robinson table bases which would be more highly respected by the structural purist.

As Charles' confidence in his own abilities and creative drive increased, he was able to convince his clients that he should design more and more of their interior furnishings. For the ultimate bungalows he was including in his work leaded stained glass, lighting fixtures, carpets, hardware, fireplace tools, garden pottery, curtains, fabrics, bookplates, and other household items as well as landscape designs.

Dining room table, David B. Gamble house, 1908.
Marvin Rand photograph.

By 1907 Emil Lange and Charles Greene had developed techniques for leaded glass fabrication which produced the effects that Charles had long been seeking. Their method allowed for greater variation in the breadth of the leading. Standard lead came was used between each piece of cut glass and the design soldered together. Sheet lead was then cut as an overlay in the pattern and dimension required. The leaf of the lead came from one side was then cut off, solder applied to the back of the sheet lead then attached to the heart of the came by heat from a medium heated soldering iron. Solder was then floated onto the entire surface of the sheet lead pattern and a copper finish achieved by chemical treatment with bluestone. To achieve the textured surface of the leading—as in the entry doors of the Gamble house—the solder was floated onto the surface of the sheet lead in individual drops giving variation in size and form when hardened. When one side of the glass was thus finished, it was turned over, the leaf of the lead came similarly removed and the process repeated in identical manner. At the same time similar processes for varying leading techniques were developed simultaneously in the east with no apparent connection with the experiments being done by the Greenes and Emil Lange. Others would follow quickly but this method of glass fabrication was so costly that its use was rare by others, particularly in residential work where it was used so effectively by Greene and Greene.[4]

Charles added a further subtlety to the best of Louis Tiffany's glass variations by laminating two, three and even four layers of glass in order to achieve the soft variations in colors to suit his particular taste. Techniques began with those used by the Tiffany Studios in New York with whom

4. Interviews with glass artisan Claus Willenberg who worked at one time in the Sturdy-Lange art glass studios in Los Angeles.

Detail of leading technique which Charles Greene and Emil Lange developed to provide greater variation and texture in the leaded glass designs.
Marvin Rand photograph.

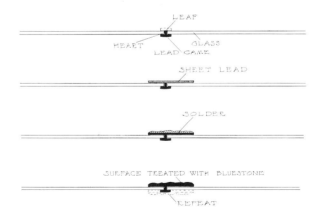

A diagram of the technique used to provide the wide range of line value and texture to the Greenes' leaded glass work.

Living room lantern and plaster relief,
Blacker house.

Lily pad motifs echoing the pond
of the garden were carried out in
the overhead stained glass lanterns
and in relief in the plaster ceiling
which was treated with an overlay
of gold leaf.

Lange had formerly been associated. Each piece of glass was wrapped with copper foil, attached one to the other with solder and molten lead, and then soft lead placed over the joints. In special instances the finished product would be acid-etched as in the veins of the leaves in the doorway of the Gamble house.

In the lighting fixtures, Charles' designs were carried out with Tiffany glass and fabricated by Lange. The glass panels were then placed into wooden or metal frames which were either affixed to the wall or hung from the ceiling with leather straps or metal rods. It is obvious that Charles took great delight in the variety and scope of lighting and was constantly searching for new ways to work with the recently developed electric technology.

In a few instances Charles was given the opportunity to design carpets, the most noteworthy of which was for the

David B. Gamble house in 1908. His watercolors for this carpet exhibit a remarkable quality of abstract composition for the times. Records are incomplete but suggest that the carpets were woven in Austria from Charles' watercolor sketches.[5] However, when they arrived in Pasadena, Charles was so dissatisfied with one of the dye colors woven into the pattern that he engaged the Iran Company in Los Angeles to unweave the one color and reweave it to his exact specifications—a job which took several weeks.

Charles was also developing the hardware for some of the ultimate bungalows. In many instances this involved

5. One letter in the Greene archives suggests that the carpets were made in England. However, Sidney Gamble, who was 18 years of age at the time the carpets were made, recalled their being woven in Austria. Notations on invoices from the Iran Company in Los Angeles refer to the 'German rugs.'

not only the metal straps for the fastening of the great timbers both inside and outside the structure, but also included andirons for fireplaces, the fireplace fenders, tools and electric switch plates. These items were manufactured by several firms in the Los Angeles area, including in 1911 the Pacific Ornamental Iron Works and by 1914 the Art Metal Company of Los Angeles. Dates of invoices from these two firms for work for the William R. Thorsen house indicate the length of time between the construction of the houses and the initial furniture and the design and production of the related designs of interior furnishings.

Charles' enthusiasm was infectious. Consequently, some of his clients encouraged him to design applique work for various fabrics used in curtains and bedspreads. The stitchery would then be carried out by the ladies and elder daughters of the families involved.

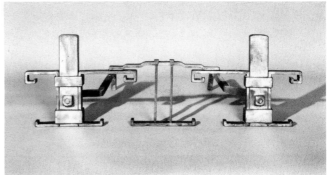

Andirons designed for Mrs. Belle Barlow Bush were made also for Peter Hall's home, circa 1910.

Peter Hall was intrigued by this innovative design which allowed for the central portion of the andiron to adjust to varying widths of the firebox by the placement of the end drop into any of several square holes in the longer arm of each andiron.

Left:
Loft lantern, Freeman A. Ford house, 1907.
Marvin Rand photographs.

The Greenes' control of the landscaping prompted Charles to design outside furniture for the terraces and the garden as well as garden pots. The pottery was produced by the Gladding-McBean Company in Lincoln, California; although in later years Charles worked with a pottery manufacturer in the San Jose area, where he actually painted the glaze patterns himself.

Glazed ceramic garden urn for the Pratt house and also utilized in the gardens of the James A. Culbertson house. Marvin Rand photograph.

During this period Charles designed a handsome large cabinet for his own office to house his fine collection of architectural drawings and publications. He was also engaged to do the interior lighting and leaded glass windows for the Earle C. Anthony residence of 1909. These windows represent some of the best stained glass window designs of his entire career.

By 1909 Charles was exhausted by the pressure of work and, consequently, he and his family visited England for a year where he relaxed, associated with writers and artists, painted in watercolors, and associated with the noted etcher, Sherbourne.[6] The fact that Charles was able to leave the practice at such a demanding and critical time is evidence of his confidence in his brother Henry, Peter and John Hall, and Emil Lange. Excerpts from an important letter from Peter Hall to Charles Greene dated August 9, 1909, are revealing:

> The Berkeley job is progressing nicely, the brick work is turning out beautifully. We have the frame up ready for shakes and I think it looks very well. We get along very nicely with Mr. Thorsen....

And in another paragraph:

> The pianos are under way and we will make at least one case from the drawing you left us. I think they will turn out very well.
>
> The Gamble House is ready to be accepted and the furniture about completed. Everything looks very well. I am well pleased with it. It will be all ready for Mr. Gamble when he arrives. The Blacker furniture is well under way

6. Interview with Charles' eldest son Nathaniel Patrickson Greene.

and is working out beautifully. It will be all ready when he arrives except the finishing which cannot be done until the inlaying is done. I forgot to mention that Mr. Blacker's electric fixtures are all done and hung and they look very well.

I have been spending most of my time lately at Berkeley. We are doing some work at Mr. Culbertsons, changing the stairway, but will not be able to finish it until you return as Mr. Culbertson wants you to design the work.

In reference to other work in the Greene office, Hall went on to write: "Your brother is getting along nicely; the work is moving along well...he has submitted several new plans and he has had bids on them, but has not gone ahead. We have figured on four different plans since you left, competition on all...." [7]

When Charles returned from England in late 1909 nearly his entire energies were focused on the interior furnishings for the ultimate bungalows. But in his own mind he felt that by this time he had done about all he could do with wood. He was also anxious to spend more time in writing, painting and other artistic endeavors.[8] It is not surprising then that he withdrew somewhat from the ordinary architectural work in the office and turned his attention to the few major commissions which offered special challenges.

Fewer and fewer opportunities came to him over the next decade, and as his own interests shifted away from the architectural practice in Pasadena, so too did the direction of his interior furnishings. Yet between 1907 and 1910 Greene and Greene had produced some of the finest furniture in America emanating from the Arts and Crafts Movement.

7. Courtesy Documents Collection, College of Environmental Design, U.C.B.

8. Interviews by the author with Nathaniel P. Greene.

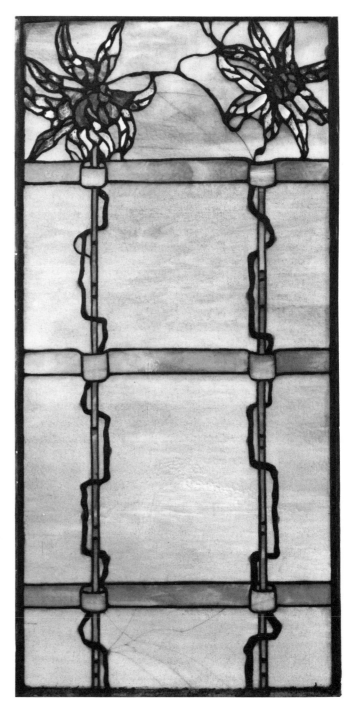

Right:
Stained glass window, Earle C. Anthony house, 1909. Marvin Rand photograph.

The window composition represents typical forms used in the Greenes' designs during the years of their most noted works.

IV

Changing Attitudes and New Directions   1911-1916

The last major commission authorizing Greene and Greene to design the total interior and furnishings was for the elaborate residence for Cordelia A. Culbertson and her two maiden sisters. They were the only clients after 1910 who had both the interest and the means to give Charles the artistic and economic freedom he demanded.

In the preceding four years the Greenes had been spoiled by the seemingly unlimited budgets provided by wealthy clients. After Charles' return from England several large residences had been designed for various clients, but they had gone no further than the drawing boards, primarily because of the high costs involved. Then, too, public tastes were changing, turning away from natural woods and leaning towards what would soon be identified as Spanish Colonial Revival. Charles himself was seeking out new materials and new forms. The scope and the unusual site of the Culbertson house was an exciting challenge, and the confidence which the three sisters had in him promised a close and satisfying working relationship.

Although the basic lines of the Culbertson furniture had the same forthright character of Charles' earlier designs, the tastes of the three ladies combined with Charles' own interest in inlay work led to distinct differences between this furniture and all others designed by the firm. Brocaded fabrics were used in upholstery, extensive etching was done in the clear glass of various cabinet pieces, and the most decorative element is to be found in the inlay work of the furniture for the entry hall.

In the latter part of 1912, the Culbertson sisters sent Charles to New York to select some furnishings in addition to those he had designed, as well as various fabrics, lighting fixtures, and other accessories for the interiors. He purchased many items for the Culbertsons and also various wall fabrics for his own house.

In an article which Charles wrote for the *Pacific Coast Architect* in March of 1914, his discussion of the furniture and interiors indicated a deep concern for the designs and furnishings of the historical past.
He wrote:

> The furniture of the hall consists of two tall back chairs of very dark crotch mahogany, inlaid with koa, lilac roots and vermillion. The design is a delicate band with twining wild roses. There is a large case or wardrobe of the corresponding design and material. Also two smaller tables at each side of the opening to the living-room. The floor covering is Bohemian hand-tufted rugs in shades of blue, with a touch of soft dull gold after a Chinese pattern. The same is in the living-room.

> The living-room furniture is of the same material, but slightly different design from the hall. The chairs and two couches are covered with silk brocade, black and gold, after an old Queen Anne pattern, in imitation of the Chinese. The walls of both rooms are covered with linen velour specially designed for hangings. The color of this and the woodwork is something near cafe au lait, but being changeable, it harmonizes well with the rugs and tones with the dull gold. There is a large desk table with a dull black marble top, delicately gold-veined. There is a bookcase and a secretary, both with glass doors. A cut design of roses suggests the inlay design of the hall pieces. There is a very delicate inlay of golden in color. In the photographic reproductions the color scale has been somewhat disarranged. Some harsh lines and contrasts that are not to be seen in the original, show disagreeably.

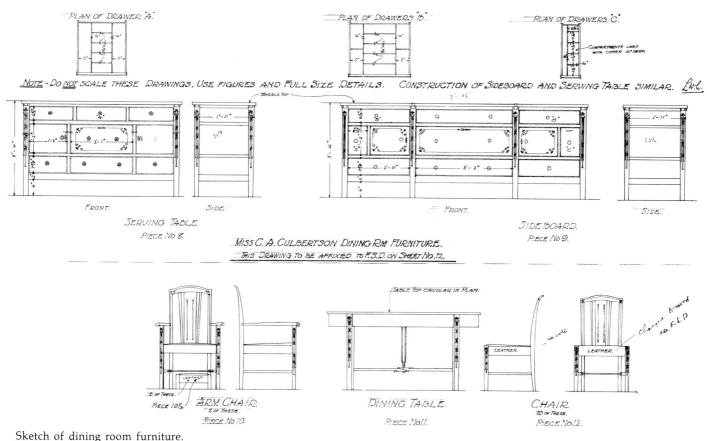

Sketch of dining room furniture.
Drawing courtesy Documents Collection,
College of Environmental Design, U.C.B.

Of the furniture in the dining room, Charles went on to write:

> This furniture is of mahogany, but light and warmer than that of the hall and living-room. The center table is round and has simple ribbon inlay in the top, which is meant to hold a small centerpiece and vase of flowers when not in use. The serving table and sideboard have tops of numidian marble, to match the panel in the mantel. The carved inlay is of oak knots, representing reeds and lotus flowers.[1]

Further in the article he discussed the various pieces of furniture which he selected rather than designed for other aspects of the house, some of which included Queen Anne carved walnut chairs and settees, Queen Anne lacquered chairs, secretary, and other pieces of the same period. He discussed the guest room furniture, which is a lacquered set; it has not yet been determined whether these pieces were designed by him or whether he selected them on his trip to New York. In the final paragraph of the article he stated very clearly that the furniture and fittings of the Culbertson house were either selected or designed and executed by the architects.

1. "Culbertson Residence, Pasadena, Cal.," *Pacific Coast Architect,* (March 1914), pp. 10, 11.

Living room desk case and chairs,
Cordelia A. Culbertson house, Pasadena, 1911.
Photograph courtesy Documents Collection,
College of Environmental Design, U.C.B.

Although the photograph is dominated by the brocade print
of the chair upholstery, the desk case has the basic directness
usually identified with the work of Charles Greene. The
large scale of the piece is gently softened by his masterful
sculptured detail in the corners and legs and by the playful
cut glass detail of the bookshelving doors.

Entry hall armoire and highback armchair. Photograph courtesy Documents Collection, College of Environmental Design, U.C.B.

Charles' personal interest in inlay and carving was given creative opportunity by the three maiden Culbertson sisters, and he exercised his imagination to the fullest.

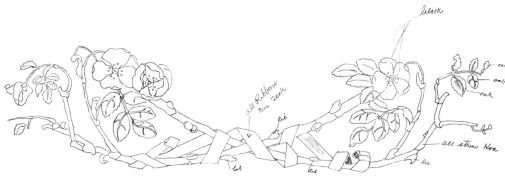

Typical detail of inlay work.
Drawing courtesy Documents Collection,
College of Envirnmental Design, U.C.B.

The careful selection of inlay woods included oak, vermillion, maple of differing colors, knurled white oak, mahogany, ebony, lignumvitae, and light colored teak.

View of dining room.
Photograph courtesy Greene and Greene Library.

Early drawings for the dining room furnishings included wall sconces, a central chandelier, and a center vase for the table—all designed to relate to the furniture. The final design featured antique lighting fixtures with molded plaster ceiling relief.

Detail of sideboard.
Marvin Rand photograph.

Marble matching the fireplace of the dining room capped the serving table and sideboard and related to the subtle colorations of the inlay detail and carved ebony drawer pulls.

Detail of wrought iron stair railing leading to the Italianate
pond of the elaborate lower gardens.
Marvin Rand photograph.

One of two identical lanterns which grace the steps at
the sidewalk.
Marvin Rand photograph.

The heavy carved copper and marble bases were designed
to complement the antique lanterns which matched those used
elsewhere in the house and on the terraces.

Charles was so completely involved in the structure and interior furnishings of the Culbertson house that he had no time to concern himself with other work in the office between 1910 and 1913. As a result Henry took almost the entire responsibility for a commission for Mrs. Parker A. Earle for an apartment house called Herkimer Arms.

The importance of the Earle apartments to the Greene story is the amount of built-in and mass-produced furniture which Henry designed and which was made by the Peter Hall mills. In addition to the built-in furniture, Henry's

sense of the curious and his concern for saving space led to a combination of overlapping uses of space within each small apartment. As the living room was also the bedroom, he placed a raised closet to the right of the entry and up two stairs. This allowed for the bed to slide out from underneath the closet. When the bed was not in use, a sliding panel could be pulled out from the wall and used as a desk. He demonstrated this same ingenuity in other aspects of the interiors of these small apartments. Each apartment had a complement of small tables, bedroom bureaus and a very

Gate leg table, Earle apartments.
Marvin Rand photographs.

The design for the gate leg table operation was unusually simple.

simple, well-designed drop-leaf circular table, all of which were mass-produced. This was the only occasion when Greene and Greene designs were made in multiple quantities. The leg structure of the drop-leaf table was so basic and fundamental that a number of furniture makers have wondered why such a direct, straightforward system for a gateleg table had not been developed by others much earlier.

Henry was also responsible for the electric lighting for the residence of Mr. and Mrs. Henry A. Ware, who wanted certain traditional English designs followed in the interiors. The major problem confronting Henry was the fact that because of poor eyesight Mrs. Ware was bothered by electric lighting fixtures. His solution was to provide indirect lighting by means of a graceful and simple wooden light trough surrounding the entire living room. Moreover, the sculptural character of the fixture and the simplicity of the way with which he joined the various lengths of the light trough demonstrate his direct but sensitive approach to the solving of awkward problems.

Parker A. Earle apartments, Pasadena, 1911.
Marvin Rand photograph.

Built-in shelving with pull-out desk encloses the raised closet under which the full-size bed is stored when not in use.

Indirect lighting detail, Henry A. Ware house, Pasadena, 1913.
Marvin Rand photograph.

Sideboard, 1913, Charles S. Greene house, Pasadena. Marvin Rand photograph.

In marked contrast to Charles' designs for clients after 1910, the unadorned simplicity of the furniture for his own home related to the firm's early designs and draws its primary beauty from the richness of scale and proportion.

Corner china case, Charles S. Greene house.
Marvin Rand photograph.

In late 1911 Charles designed one of the first pieces of the more refined furniture for his own home—a rosewood writing desk. Late in 1912 he designed additional pieces, including chairs, writing tables, dining table, sideboard, and a particularly interesting corner china cabinet, all of which were made at the Peter Hall mill. What was most interesting about the furniture for his own home was the dramatic simplicity in contrast to the elaborately decorative work being done at the same time for the Culbertson sisters. Perhaps Charles' deference to his clients explains the variance of designs from one client to another while the simplicity of his own furniture suggests that he himself preferred to live with more direct and simpler pieces of furniture. It is also possible that the simplicity of his own furniture was influenced as much by cost as by taste. At the same time some of his designs for later clients indicate his fascination with intricate inlay work and complex floral compositions in folded ribbon patterns worked into soft plaster.

Between 1907 and 1909 Charles developed a signature which he would woodburn into the underside or sometimes even on the exposed portion of his furniture. The family of Mrs. Belle Barlow Bush clearly recalled that some time after the furniture had been delivered, Charles came by one day with his tools and woodburned his signature into each of the pieces he had designed for the Bush household.[2]

On May 27, 1912 Charles filed an application with the United States Patent Office for registration of a trademark.

It was about this time that Charles Greene dropped the name Charles and began to go by his middle name alone until he moved to Carmel where his stationery and signature became C. Sumner Greene.

2. Correspondence with Mrs. Beatrice Barlow Bissell.

To all whom it may concern:

Be it known that I, SUMNER GREENE, a citizen of the United States of America, residing at Pasadena, county of Los Angeles, State of California, and doing business at 215–232 Boston Building, in said city, have adopted and used the trade-mark shown in the accompanying drawing, being my fac-simile signature, no claim being made to the words "His True Mark," for furniture, in Class No. 32, Furniture and upholstery, as follows: chairs, tables, stands, commodes, lounges, davenports, sofas, bedsteads, dress-

ers, looking-glass frames, sideboards, book-cases, desks, hat-racks, cabinets, stools, benches, piano-cases, piano benches and stools.

The trade-mark has been continuously used in my business since November 30, 1910.

The trade-mark is applied or affixed to the goods, or to the packages containing the same, by branding on some portion of each article with a red hot metal brand, and is my signature.

SUMNER GREENE.

Trade-mark document for furniture and upholstery, February 3, 1914.
Courtesy Greene and Greene Library.

Woodburned into visible areas of the furniture, this signature was utilized inconsistently and for a very short period of time.

The one other major commission between 1911 and 1915 on which Charles was working was the large residence and estate of Mr. and Mrs. Mortimer Fleishhacker in Wood-side, California. No furniture was initially designed for this house, but the association with the Fleishhackers did result in designs for alterations to the Fleishhacker residence in San Francisco. Designs were begun in 1914 and were carried on for several years. Although some of the designs for the San Francisco house were never carried out, particularly those for the furniture, the drawings indicate a similar ornate character to the furniture as that for the Culbertson sisters in 1911. This concern for complex ornament, folded patterns and historical motifs was not only evident in the furniture designs but also in wall lighting sconces, moldings and plaster reliefs. Similar to the interiors for the Culbertson sisters, the design sketches are very elaborate and included swagged draperies of heavy fabrics with bold valances and a total conceptual development of the entire interior space. Charles was obviously eager to do the entire job; however, only portions of it were carried out.

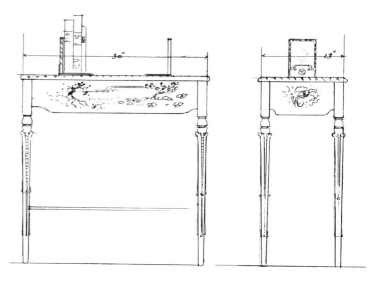

Sketches for furniture project for Fleishhacker San Francisco house.
Drawing courtesy Documents Collection, College of Environmental Design, U.C.B.

Charles harmonizes the plasticity of his intricate plaster relief designs with the detail carvings and shaping of the furniture in wood.

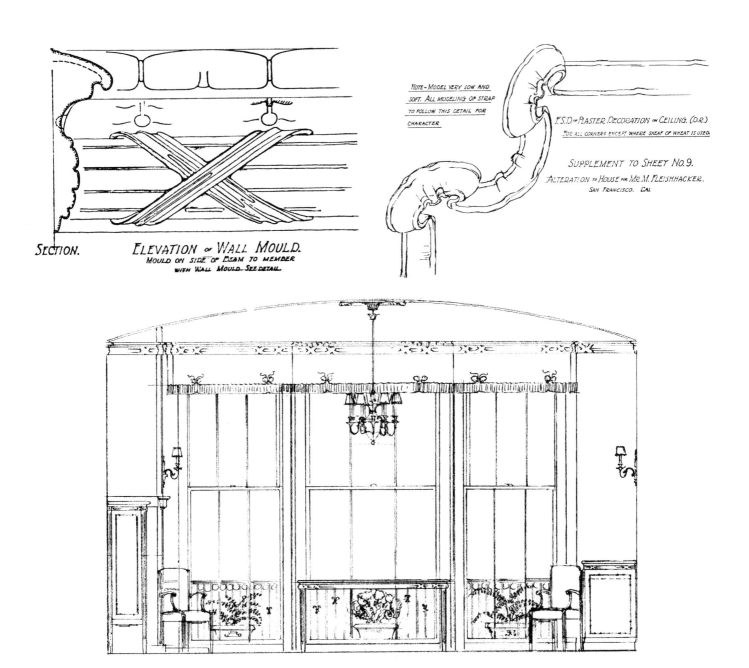

SECTION.

ELEVATION OF WALL MOULD.
MOULD ON SIDE OF BEAM TO MEMBER
WITH WALL MOULD. SEE DETAIL

NOTE—MODEL VERY LOW AND
SOFT. ALL MODELING OF STRAP
TO FOLLOW THIS DETAIL FOR
CHARACTER

F.S.D. OF PLASTER DECORATION ON CEILING. (D.R.)
FOR ALL CORNERS EXCEPT WHERE SHEAF OF WHEAT IS USED.

SUPPLEMENT TO SHEET NO. 9.
ALTERATION TO HOUSE FOR MR. M. FLEISHHACKER.
SAN FRANCISCO. CAL

Preliminary sketch for interior remodeling, Mortimer Fleishhacker house, (designed by others), San Francisco, 1915. Drawings courtesy Documents Collection, College of Environmental Design, U.C.B.

The architectural work was carried on for several years in plaster relief designs and cut glass windows. The furniture was never made; however, its design sketches are very similar to the armchair which Charles later made for the game room for the Fleishhacker home in 1923.

Shortly before Charles decided to move his family to Carmel, Mr. Gamble and the residents along Westmoreland Place had been plagued with tourist busses driving along their private street. As a result they commissioned the Greenes to close one end of Westmoreland Place and to design and place signs at both ends indicating that Westmoreland Place was a private and not a through street and that it was not accessible to company bus tours. The end result was a beautiful composition of boulder piers at Rosemont, formerly Lester Avenue, and the furnishing of Westmoreland Place with wrought iron gates with the same movement and grace as the wrought iron work in the Earle C. Anthony Auto Showroom of 1911 and in the gates to the portals of Oaklawn done in 1906. The signs on Westmoreland Place exhibited a playful but serious typeface selection and were suspended from a wooden structure which related to the two Greene and Greene houses nearby—the Gamble house and John Addison Cole house. At the same time, in developing the open end of Westmoreland Place, Charles had divided the entrance and exit around a majestic deodar tree. In later letters to Henry he expressed a great disappointment that the lines of the street were not adhered to in the actual construction by Mr. Gamble and the other residents.[3]

As less and less work came into the office after 1911, Charles grew more and more attracted to the life-style of the people around Carmel—the painters, writers, poets and photographers with whom he enjoyed associating. During his visits to the Fleishhacker job site in Woodside, he had visited Carmel several times and eventually on June 2, 1916 he and his family moved there. This date marks the beginning of the end of an era for the Greenes, although the actual dissolution of the firm did not take place until 1922.

Charles and Henry continued their great respect and affection for each other, but they recognized that their individual desires were diverging and leading down different paths. Though there would be occasions where the brothers worked together on new projects for previous clients, the years of semi-practice and semi-retirement for Greene and Greene is now a story of each of the brothers independent of the other.

3. Correspondence from Charles Greene to Henry Greene in April 1917.

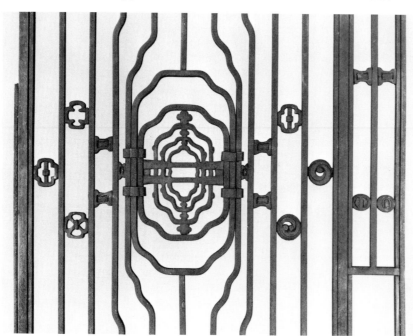

Left:
Elevator detail of wrought iron work,
Earle C. Anthony Automobile Showroom,
Los Angeles, 1911.
Marvin Rand photograph.

Similar designs were utilized in the balcony railings, stairway housing, and entrance doors and canopy.

Gates and portals of Westmoreland Place, Pasadena, 1916. Marvin Rand photograph.

The Tanner Livery Company would frequently bring tours through Westmoreland Place in open vehicles and drivers would extoll the virtues of Pasadena living over megaphones. The distractions eventually prompted David Gamble and the other residents to engage the Greenes to close off one end of the private street to through traffic and to place signs at the entrance indicating the street was private property.

V

C. Sumner Greene — The Later Years   1916-1934

After Charles Greene moved to Carmel his work on interiors and furnishings was commissioned primarily by former clients or new owners of the large residences completed in earlier years. At the time of the move Charles was completing work on a significant lamp design for the Culbertsons, and was deeply involved with the work for Mr. and Mrs. Mortimer Fleishhacker in San Francisco. Correspondence in December of 1916 indicated that eleven men were working on the job at that time.[1] While this did not involve furniture it did involve a great deal of detailed work on the molded and carved plaster relief in the interior of the space and in the marble carvings for mantels and other details.

Early in 1917 Charles first heard from Henry that the Culbertson sisters were considering the sale of their house. It was purchased on April 29, 1917 by Mrs. Dudley P. Allen. She was so impressed by Charles' designs of the interiors and furnishings of the house that within a week she had travelled up to Pebble Beach to discuss with him the design of further furnishings. According to Charles' correspondence, Mrs. Allen ordered sketches for a screen and two mirrors for the dining room, marble jardinieres for the hall, another lamp for the living room, and a piano case for the garden room. Over the years both Charles and Henry Greene developed a good working relationship with her, and she highly valued the subtleties of Charles' workmanship. Although there would be a great deal of work with Mrs. Allen within the next decade, at times there were difficulties in communication and misunderstandings about

deliveries and costs, many of which were created by Charles. As early as July 5, 1917, just a few weeks after meeting Mrs. Allen, Charles wrote:

> I have been waiting for word from Mrs. Allen, but as I have not heard I think she must be away. If you think it necessary, I will come down even if I don't hear from her. It is such a job to get figures on her work at a distance. Everybody is afraid of it or me. I am out of patience with people who must have figures as if they would make the work any cheaper. However, I hope she will let me do the work; it would be a great help to me just now.

In another letter to the office in Pasadena, Charles wrote on June 27:

> If Mrs. Allen would only decide to do something, I could come down there and help Hal out, but otherwise it is so expensive.

With reference to Charles' writing that was in process in Carmel at the time, he writes further:

> My story has been sadly neglected lately since I commenced Mrs. Allen's furniture drawings, but just now they are off my hands for a few days until John Hall can figure some of it. I won't have much respite though.[2]

1. Correspondence from C. Sumner Greene to his father in December, 1916. Courtesy of Robert Judson Clark and Documents Collection, College of Environmental Design, U.C.B.
2. Excerpts of Charles Greene's correspondence, courtesy Robert Judson Clark.

By September, however, all problems had been resolved and Charles was moving ahead on the furniture designs for Mrs. Allen. These included an attachable round top as well as a rectangular top which could be attached to the dining table designed earlier for the Culbertson sisters. The attachments for the alternate additional tops were so intricate that Charles even designed the hardware used to install and stabilize them. By September 10 John Hall had been authorized to do the more expensive table top. Work proceeded swiftly and some of the items, such as the mirrors for the dining room, were delivered to Mrs. Allen as early as October.

In 1908 Mrs. Allen remarried and became Mrs. Frances F. Prentiss, and it was under this name that the house was frequently published over the years. Charles did numerous drawings for dining room screens and the piano lamp which she had ordered. The drawings for the lamp indicate his concern for the most minute detail in the forming of the cast bronze of the bases and reveal a sophistication and concern for form which was very much akin to the graceful designs of Louis Comfort Tiffany for his lamp bases. The full-size detail drawings for the dining room screen exhibit a similar sophistication and concern for detail. Although there were numerous preliminary sketches of various designs for the piano, none of them were carried through to a final design, and the piano probably was never made.

Charles' account books indicate that he continued work-

C. Sumner Greene, 1934.
Photograph by Henry Greene,
courtesy Greene and Greene Library.

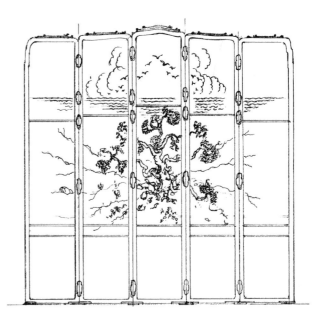

Folding screen for dining room, (Cordelia Culbertson home) for Mrs. Dudley P. Allen (later Mrs. Francis F. Prentiss), 1917.
Drawing courtesy Documents Collection,
College of Environmental Design, U.C.B.

Above:
Table lamp for the Culbertson sisters, 1916.

Shortly before the sale of the house to Mrs.
Dudley P. Allen in April, 1917, the Culbertson
sisters commissioned Charles to design a
table lamp for the living room which combined
an antique oriental urn with fixture design and
shade paintings by Charles.

Above left, left:
Piano lamp for living room for Mrs. Dudley
P. Allen, 1917.
Photographs courtesy Documents Collection,
College of Environmental Design, U.C.B.

Shade and base details were designed to
coordinate with the lamp done for the Culbertson sisters the previous year.

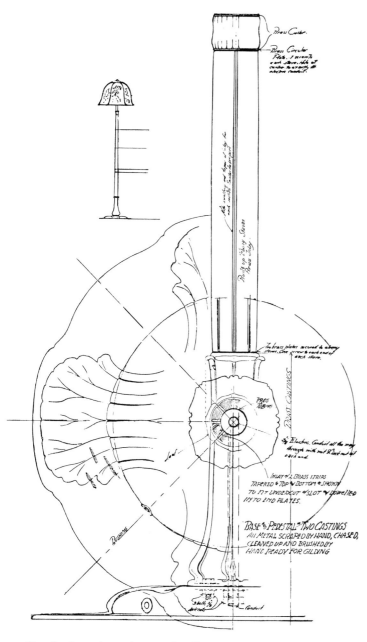

Detail of cast brass base and collars with stem of ebony
staves with brass inlay for Allen piano lamp.
Drawing courtesy Documents Collection,
College of Environmental Design, U.C.B.

ing for Mrs. Prentiss through 1920. Accounts for April 1919
and February 1920 indicate payments of as much as $3000
for panels. The nature of these panels and where they were
placed is unknown as these do not appear to be the carved
and painted plaques made for the dining room some seven
years later. The 1920 entries record expenses for a trip to
Los Angeles in connection with the Prentiss furniture, although the pieces of furniture were not identified. It is quite
possible that there was a break in the relationship between
Charles and Mrs. Prentiss around 1920, for the records
show that Henry Greene was designing furniture for Mrs.
Prentiss in 1925, and it was not until 1926 that Charles again
became actively involved in further work for Mrs. Prentiss.

In 1917, about the time he started on the initial work for
Mrs. Prentiss, Charles was also commissioned by Mr. and
Mrs. Henry M. Robinson to add several pieces to their
earlier furniture. This also included the enclosure of a side
porch for a game room. The wooden carvings in the paneling of this room reflected the sculptural character of the
plaster relief resembling that done for the Fleishhacker's
San Francisco house the year before. The following year
the Robinsons commissioned a tea table and lamp which
was very similar to the design of a floor lamp developed as
the piano lamp for Mrs. Prentiss.

Detail of carved marble mantel, D. L. James house.
Marvin Rand photograph.

The marble carvings were done in San Francisco and relate to other wooden patterns which Charles carved.

In addition to work for former clients, Charles was deeply involved in work on the D.L. James house in Carmel Highlands. In a letter of September 22, 1921 discussing an adjustment of architectural fees, there is a reference to furniture and fixtures on the same 6 percent basis. Drawings indicate Charles' eagerness to design the furniture for the James house. One such drawing was for a white oak desk somewhat similar to his previous work, but showing considerably more sculptural carving in the wood. This marks a departure from Charles' previous furniture as here he was emphasizing carved form rather than the natural grain of the wood or the inlaid patterns. According to their son, Daniel, the Jameses felt that Charles' furniture was much too light for their taste. They preferred more massive antiques in the house and subsequently selected seventeenth century Italian and English pieces.[3]

In 1923 Charles began work on his own studio in Carmel. Here the carvings for the timbers of the living room, various beams for door openings, the carved doors and a large bookcase designed for the studio demonstrate the continuing strength and versatility of his creative imagination.

3. Interviews with Daniel and Lilith James.

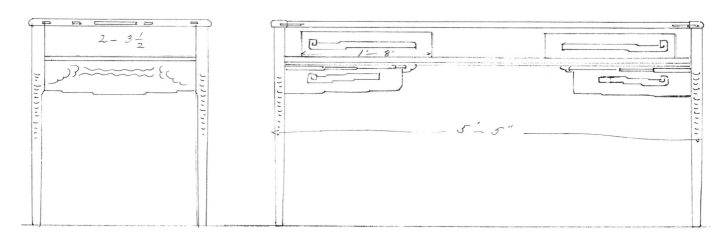

Sketch for proposed furniture for D. L. James house,
Carmel Highlands, 1918-1923.
Drawing courtesy Documents Collection,
College of Environmental Design, U.C.B.

The design of white oak was too light in scale for Mr. and Mrs. James who eventually furnished the house in European antique pieces.

Elaborately carved entry door,
C. Sumner Greene studio,
Carmel-by-the-sea, 1923.
Marvin Rand photograph.

The carved exterior of the solid
teakwood door is an interesting
contrast with the elegant linear
simplicity of the inside face.

Interior of C. Sumner Greene's studio showing the large bookcase designed for his office
in the Boston Building in Pasadena during the era of the work on the elaborate bungalows.
Roy Flamm photograph.

Detail of bookcase.
Marvin Rand photograph.

The carvings in wood are again representative of Charles' preoccupation with the plasticity of his designs in plaster relief for the Fleishhackers, Jameses, and in his own studio.

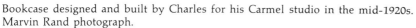

Bookcase designed and built by Charles for his Carmel studio in the mid-1920s.
Marvin Rand photograph.

Built of inexpensive low grade woods, Charles painted the surface which he treated and rubbed as though working with a lacquer finish.

Interior of the small office in Charles' Carmel studio.
Roy Flamm photograph.

Three distinct eras of Charles Greene's designs are represented here: the very early Stickley-influenced plain oak filing cabinet which Charles built in 1903 in the shop behind his Pasadena home; the mahogany cabinet to the left relating to the furniture from the elaborate bungalow years (1907-1911); and the sculptured treatment of forms and space of his later studies.

Entry hall of the Carmel studio.
Roy Flamm photograph.

Detail of French door between entry and main room of Carmel studio.
Marvin Rand photograph.

This excellent door was never completed and still exhibits the sequence of Charles' wood carving from pencil and chalk initial ideas to the nearly completed carving.

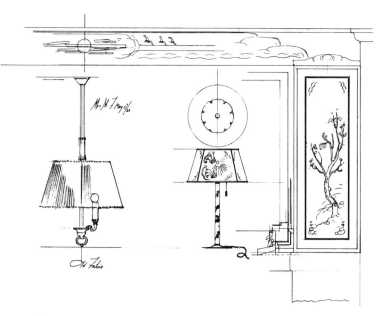

In 1923 Mr. and Mrs. Mortimer Fleishhacker again called on Charles, this time to enclose a side porch of their residence at Woodside as a game room. The commission was quickly accepted for Charles was not only in need of work, but still eager to do further work on the Fleishhacker house at Woodside and to design furniture for that house. The game room was fully crafted by Charles; it was the only room in the house developed in natural woods, and it was the first time in over two decades that he actually had an opportunity to make client's furniture himself. He had developed a woodshop next to his studio in Carmel. The

Sketch of proposals for the Fleishhacker game room.
Drawing courtesy Documents Collection,
College of Environmental Design, U.C.B.

Forms in this drawing for the frieze are more typical of the finished carvings; however, the cabinet door sketch is less contrived here. The chandelier and table lamp were never constructed.

Right:
Corner of game room interior added to Mortimer Fleishhacker house, Woodside, California, 1923.
Marvin Rand photograph.

The linearity of the French doors relates the converted open porch space to the character of the original design of the house in 1911. Charles' interest in stylistic abstraction in his carvings dominates the interiors in the many cabinet doors, wooden friezes, furniture, and in the patterns pressed into the soft plaster of the walls and ceiling.

combination of the carvings for the paneling, the doors to cabinets, the game table, four chairs and arm chair took over two years to complete. The similarity in the design for the furniture of this game room and the proposed sketches for the furniture for the D. L. James house was an indication of Charles' determination to carry out his new ideas regarding the sculptural quality of carvings in the furniture of the early twenties.

In addition to the paneling and furniture, Charles' designs made it necessary for him to make the instruments with which he tooled the leather of the upholstery and the leather top of the game table which were then accented with color and leather glaze. The Fleishhacker game room furniture is a good example of the major role which John Hall played in the detail and construction of furniture. Without John Hall's expertise and without the proper equipment of the mill the joinery of the furniture for the Fleishhackers was less sophisticated. Such devices as a simple metal clip screwed to the top and the edge of the table were utilized in the Fleishhacker furniture in the same manner as in the very early furniture designed for the Adelaide Tichenor house in 1904.

Table and chairs for Fleishhacker game room photographed in Charles' Carmel studio.
Photograph courtesy Greene and Greene Library.

In 1925 Charles made the acquaintance of Martin Flavin, a prominent writer associated with MGM Studios. Flavin had recently had a large home designed by another architect built on Spindrift Road below Carmel Highlands overlooking the rocky coast of the Pacific Ocean. Over the years he engaged Charles in numerous projects which he later described as giving the home all of the fine character that it possessed.[4] The initial work for Flavin involved the design of a table in 1925. Between 1925 and 1930 Charles' work for Flavin consisted primarily of architectural projects, but in 1930 drawings were begun for a special private library which Flavin would use for his writing. The interior was entirely of redwood. Charles himself carved all of the panels and installed the paneling, the bookshelves and the ceiling. He designed a desk and a chair for the room as well as moveable hanging hammered copper reading light fixtures, and special lighting fixtures with handles which hung on the wall and could be lifted from their mounts and carried along the shelves to aid in the search of a particular book. Charles' carvings for Martin Flavin also included the major door between the living room and the new library, a significant large redwood relief over the fireplace mantel in the living room, and the mantel supports.

4. Correspondence to the author.

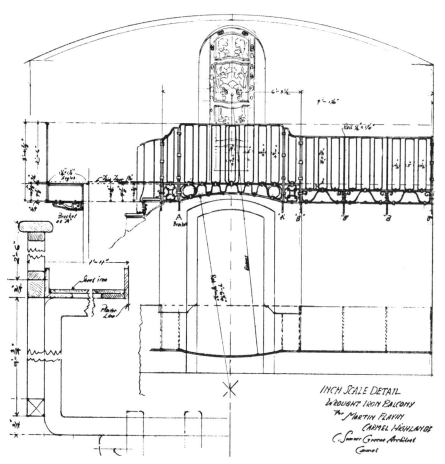

Drawing courtesy Documents Collection, College of Environmental Design, U.C.B.

View from living room into library, Martin Flavin house, Carmel Highlands, 1931. Marvin Rand photograph.

Detail of moveable hammered copper hand lamp in the
Flavin library.
Marvin Rand photograph.

One of three swinging reading lamps in the Flavin library.
Marvin Rand photograph.

Tooled leather bedroom screen for Mrs. Francis F. (Allen) Prentiss, 1926.
Photograph courtesy Greene and Greene Library.

Carved marble entry urns for Mrs. Francis F. Prentiss, 1927.
Marvin Rand photograph.

Early in 1927 Charles again was doing a considerable amount of work for Mrs. Prentiss. There had also been some work in 1926 related to another elaborate screen for Mrs. Prentiss' bedroom. However, one of the major projects which ultimately became a point of controversy between Charles and Mrs. Prentiss was the request for a series of nine carved and colored panels to be placed around the dining room. To Mrs. Prentiss the dining room seemed unfinished and upon her request Charles prepared sketches which were shipped to Mrs. Prentiss on February 9, 1927. The extent of the work for Mrs. Prentiss in 1927 and the variety of Charles' involvement is best understood through the reading of the correspondence between Charles and his brother Henry. In a letter dated June 9, 1927, Henry wrote:

> I have just received a short letter from Mrs. Prentiss in which she says if you would have the tea table, the screen, the lights for the entry hall, and the ornaments for the front entrance completed, she might give you a little lee-way on some of the panels for the dining room, but that she would not want to have to wait until the end of the season for them ... she surely has made all concessions, and it is now up to you to stick with the things and get them out for her and avoid any further disappointment to her.

On December 14 Henry wrote:

> I believe if you can get those ornaments for the front entrances here and get the three panels for the dining room here and hung, she will feel all right.

Henry to Charles on January 27, 1928:

> Mrs. Prentiss called me on the telephone just a few moments ago and asked me to write to you not to do anything more on the panels you are making for the dining room. She says, quite frankly, she does not like them. She says they are not at all what she expected—she thought that you would do something that would just blend in with the walls, but these three panels that you have hung look spotty and disturb the harmony that she felt in the room before. She rather criticizes you for not letting her know costs and doing something so she would understand a little better what was to be done before doing it. I do not know what is wrong unless it is your method of doing things.

On January 9, 1928 Mrs. Prentiss received a bill for the amount of $1,551.30 from the marble carver for his work in making the two marble vases to stand beside the front entrance. In response to the bill, she wrote to Charles on February 9, 1928 as follows:

> I need not say, perhaps, that I am rather astonished at the size of the bill for the two jars. It really had never occurred to me that they would reach such a sum, and though, of course, I did not ask you for an estimate, or you, perhaps, said you could not give one, I should have requested it before carrying on with the work. However, that is completed and they must necessarily stand. I think they are very attractive, but I must say that if I have you do any future work for me, I must request an estimate of the cost because everything that has been done recently has been a good bit beyond my expectations.
>
> With regard to the plaques in the dining room I am still of the opinion that they are not an asset, but are rather a detraction from the beauty of the room. I cannot visualize them with the color eliminated as ornamental, and I think that we shall just have to eliminate them entirely. They are so utterly different from what I had expected that I do not see how I can use them in any part of my house, and I think that I shall have to return them to you expecting that you can use them elsewhere. If it seems just to you that I should pay for the cost of material, I will be glad to do so. Otherwise it seems to me that you may have to, perhaps, stand the loss.

Charles responded to Mrs. Prentiss on February 15:

> Thank you for your check for $1,916.75 in full for urns at front entrance 1188 Hillcrest Avenue.
>
> I am both sorry and pained to know that you are dissatisfied with the cost of this year's work. Speaking of estimates, it seems to me that you do not know or have forgotten that your house and all in it were completed without an estimate and exceeded all expectation.
>
> But your fine discriminating sense singled it out from many others. Won't you believe that this was the reason? It seems plain to me.
>
> There is nothing reckless or extravagant about the work. No artist can figure original work for only one set of objects, even the factory can't; but the factory multiplies sets so that the original cost is only a fraction of the cost of each set sold.
>
> If you had come to me to build the house, but had limited me to an estimate, 1188 Hillcrest could never have existed. Business, I admit must run upon business lines, but this is not business, this art of helping to make living pleasurable and beautiful beyond the merely useful.
>
> As for the plaques, I think you have forgotten your encouraging letter of February 28, 1927, in which you gave me the order for the nine plaques...do you think it fair or business-like to simply reject them? It is far from my

Three preliminary sketches for nine proposed panels for the dining room for Mrs. Prentiss, 1926.
Drawings courtesy Greene and Greene Library.

intent to force anything on you that you do not like, but with changed and softened colors you would get the effect of restfullness that you expect. This I am not only willing but anxious to do. I am sorry that I forgot at the time your particular feeling for color, but I have already given the reason.

Please remember that I have tried to fill your order for these plaques in good faith and have spent months of my time on them.

Mrs. Prentiss replied in March, 1928:

I have thought long and carefully concerning the matters in your recent letter and while you are quite right about my words of approval of your designs for the panels in the dining room, I have to confess that the panels have not quite come up to my expectation.

As I have studied them, I just cannot see them in any altered shape or color in that room, and as the room is so perfect without them I think that we shall have to let the matter drop and I shall let you send the bill to me for those ones completed. I may be able to find a place down in the loggia for them.

On March 26, 1928 Charles wrote to Henry:

I have settled with Mrs. Prentiss and she says the three plaques are to go in the loggia. I am thoroughly disappointed, but it can't be helped. I feel that the plaques are as good as anything I have ever done and the dining room will always seem unfinished to me.

...If I thought they were defective or were not up to the standard of my work I would not have charged a cent for them. Well! That's that, and I suppose that it is the last I shall hear from her, but I think she is not malicious in the least and the things may win her back when she sees them long enough. I should never have overlooked her taste for color if they had not hurried me to the point of desperation.

In spite of the disagreements there was a genuine close relationship between Mrs. Prentiss and the Greenes, and the letter from Henry to Charles of February 11, 1929 is illustrative of that attitude. Henry wrote:

I have seen Mrs. Prentiss once or twice since she returned to Pasadena on January 15, and the first time I was out I was in her bedroom and she remarked that she loved the screens you made for her.

...She liked the style of the screen, but did not like the style of the panels. I knew that you would be interested to hear this.

In the upper left-hand corner of the letter Charles' notation indicates his persistence. It states: "Answer February 19, 1929, ask Mrs. P. to let me recolor plaques."[5]

Other works demanding Charles' attention in 1928 and 1929 involved the design of a fountain for Mr. and Mrs. Robert Blacker for their home in Pasadena, and sketches for bookcases in the entry hall, although these were never completed. Also, as part of the development of the grounds and water gardens for the Mortimer Fleishhackers, Charles was directly involved in the design of many of the garden pots and more than two hundred urns which were made by the Garden City Pottery in San Jose. Charles was continually visiting the potter and painted the patterned glaze on the pots himself.

5. Correspondence related to Mrs. Prentiss courtesy of Robert Judson Clark and Greene and Greene Library.

Fountain for rear garden, Robert R. Blacker house, Pasadena, 1928.

Marvin Rand photograph.

Above:
Ceramic garden pot for Mortimer
Fleishhacker estate, Woodside, 1928.

Right:
Stone urn for water gardens, Mortimer
Fleishhacker estate, 1927.
Marvin Rand photographs.

Charles' artistic enthusiasm and lack of proper communication with clients created a similar series of misunderstandings with Mrs. Thomas Verner Moore who had commissioned a small stool for her son. Mrs. Moore had been making the cover for the seat herself and wrote to Charles on April 11, 1930:

> I have been hoping to hear from you about when the stool is to be ready. The work I was doing is ready to send. I should like to have the stool ready to give my son on Mother's Day....I like to give my son a little remembrance that day...the price will be all right, so you don't need to let me know how much the cost is before you have it done.

However, after the stool was delivered, she wrote to Charles on December 29:

> When I saw you in Carmel I thought you were to make a very plain, but strong stool. I thought that it was to be of oak which would suit the furniture in my son's den. I told you it was a piece of his mother's work to be used in his den, so he could enjoy sitting in front of the fire for a smoke. As I said to you when I saw the beautiful work on it, that it was far too elaborate for the purpose it was to be used for. Then if the price you mentioned is correct, I was so astonished when you told me. That is prohibitive. I could not pay the amount you said. So I don't know that I can do anything else but send it back.
>
> P.S. Of course there is no use sending a seat without my work on it so please let me have the bill for the work done on that.[6]

Following further correspondence the stool was returned and kept in Charles' own possession.

Shortly thereafter Charles was commissioned by Mrs. Willis Walker to design a three-panel teakwood screen for her home. This screen was elaborately carved, but was not accepted by Mrs. Walker, probably because of its cost. That too remained in Charles' home the balance of his life.

6. Correspondence courtesy of Robert Judson Clark and Documents Collection, College of Environmental Design, U.C.B.

C. Sumner Greene with folding carved teakwood screen designed and made by him for Mrs. Willis Walker, 1934.
R. L. Makinson photograph.

Detail of one of the nine carved panels of the Walker screen. Marvin Rand photograph.

Stool for Mrs. Thomas Verner Moore, 1930. Marvin Rand photograph.

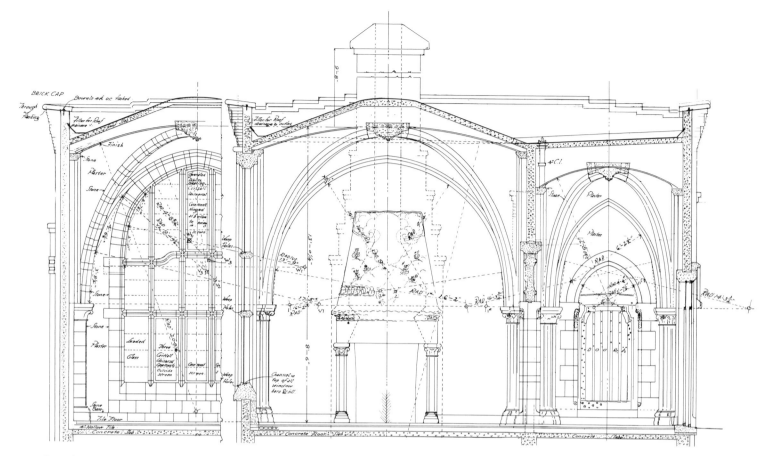

Late design of gothic room addition project for San Francisco home of Mr. and Mrs. Mortimer Fleishhacker, 1929-1932. Drawing courtesy Documents Collection, College of Environmental Design, U.C.B.

Elements from the Greenes' early architectural vocabulary and Charles' later sculptural period are intermixed in this attempted gothic design.

In the late 1920s and through 1930 and 1931 Mr. and Mrs. Mortimer Fleishhacker engaged Charles to make an addition to their San Francisco residence. This has become known as the Gothic room project and in Charles' own words presented the greatest challenge and was the hardest work he ever attempted in his life. Creation was becoming more difficult. Numerous sketches were done, many drawings carried well into refined stages, and the total development of the interiors attempted.

In early 1930 letters to Henry discussed the working drawings for the Gothic room. In November there was a reference to the plans being done. However, a letter from Charles in December indicates that they were still un-

finished. In February of 1931 Charles wrote that he was seeing daylight on the plans for the Gothic room. In June of 1931 he was taking estimates for the stonework, the woodwork, and the wrought iron for the vaulting. By mid-August Charles wrote to Henry that "some of our earlier schemes for the Gothic room have looked as hopeless as this, but between us, I expect, we will find a way out."[7]

Unfortunately, the project, in spite of the countless hours of planning, never entered construction. That is particularly unfortunate inasmuch as some of the drawings reveal a very sensitive weaving together of traditional Gothic forms

7. *Ibid.*

and recognizable characteristics of earlier Greene and Greene work. These were so carefully woven together that the end product would certainly have been one of the most unusual spaces ever created by either of the brothers.

The last few pieces of furniture Charles Greene produced by his own hands were made in the 1930s and included the stool for Mrs. Moore, the very handsome screen for Mrs. Walker, and a small table for his son, Thomas Gordon Greene and his wife. Possibly the last work was an incomplete cabinet for his wife, Alice, in which he playfully designed and carved various forms of animal life.

From the first to the last of Charles Greene's furniture designs, the basic form of the piece was of primary importance. The variation and detail of decorative elements depended upon his particular feelings at the time, his judgment of the client's wishes, and the particular era in which he was working. His personal fascination with carving revealed itself most often when he had plenty of time on his hands. It is, nevertheless, significant that the designs for his own home represent some of the purest, most direct, beautifully scaled and proportioned compositions of his entire career. The versatility, imagination, craftsmanship, and sensitivity which Charles brought to his furniture, his lighting fixtures, leaded glass designs, metal work, and all facets of the joinery, hinging, and mechanical apparatus were all given his undivided attention and all retain that certain continuity of spirit which distinguishes the furniture and related designs of Charles Sumner Greene.

Detail of one of four carved panels of a cabinet never completed for Charles' wife, Alice, circa 1934.
Roy Flamm photograph.

VI

Henry Mather Greene — The Later Years   1916-1930

Henry Greene's interest in the design of furniture and related designs began at the same time as Charles' when both were introduced to and embraced the principles of the Arts and Crafts Movement around 1902 and 1903. The demands of the firm, the necessity to administer the business of the office, the supervision of the work, and the coordination of the vast amount of activity engaged in by the firm, made it impossible for Henry to fully pursue his interests in designing furniture. It seems clear, though, when studying the furniture designs emanating from the firm between 1903 and 1906 that Henry's association is more clearly felt than with the furniture and interior designs after 1906.

During the period of the construction of the ultimate bungalows and their full complement of furniture and related designs, Henry, Peter Hall, John Hall and Emil Lange were completely immersed in the execution of the work while Charles was concentrating all his energies on the designs. The first of Henry Greene's furniture designs is a rough sketch for a round dining table and chairs for his own home. Only the chairs were made. However, it is most likely related to the period shortly following the Tichenor house of 1904 and preceding the refinements of the furniture following 1906. The design reflects Gustav Stickley's designs, although the lift form was already apparent.

The first of Henry's furniture designs made for clients appears to be in the period of the designs for Mrs. Belle Barlow Bush. There were two tables, one of which was similar in design to certain pieces for Mrs. Bush. On the back of a photograph of one of these tables, Charles noted that the table was designed by "Hal." There is no further identification as for whom the table was designed, and Henry's family has no recollection of such a table, although they believe that Henry had designed such items as bookshelves and built-in cabinets in his own home in Pasadena.[1]

Aside from furniture, there are several instances, particularly of skylight design and window design, which bear the decided imprint of Henry Greene's compositional abilities. Henry's sense of order and discipline was more likely to result in direct designs generally composed of straight lines arranged in vertical and horizontal compositions. This was exhibited in the 1902 windows for the living room of the James Culbertson house, and particularly well-handled in the direct and graceful glass compositions of the skylights for the residences for William W. Spinks and Dr. S. S. Crow in 1909.

Despite the disciplined nature of Henry's compositions, there was a playful sense in some of his designs—as in the china cabinets for the dining room and in the book cabinets for the living room of the Annie Blacker house of 1912. Henry's designs reflect the methodical, systematic order with which he conducted his entire life. He was somewhat of an amateur inventor; he was challenged by unusual situations and by the need for new technology. He was often brilliant in solving problems, as in the lighting system for Mr. and Mrs. Henry A. Ware discussed earlier.

1. Interviews by the author with Henry Dart Greene, Isabelle Greene McElwain and William Sumner Greene.

In 1915 Henry designed several pieces of furniture for an addition for the house of Dr. R. P. McReynolds. However, there is no record that this furniture was ever made.

In 1918, after Charles had moved to Carmel, Henry was involved in the addition to a structure designed by others for Mr. John Whitworth in Altadena. In the course of this job, he designed several pieces of furniture, bathroom cabinets, and wall lighting fixtures for the bedroom wing. These designs suggested earlier forms utilized in the Greenes' designs combined with a feeling for some of the characteristics related to the popular Spanish Colonial Revival.

Henry Mather Greene, 1924.
Photograph courtesy Greene and Greene Library.

Leaded clear glass china case doors, Annie Blacker house, Pasadena, 1912.
R. L. Makinson photograph.

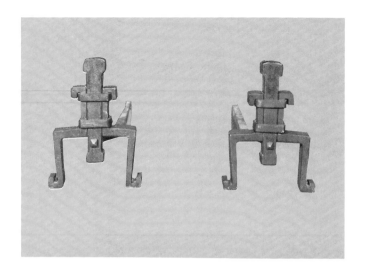

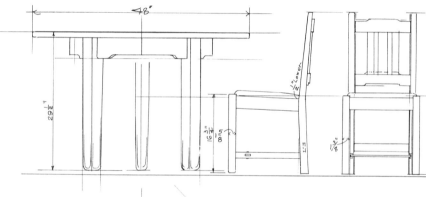

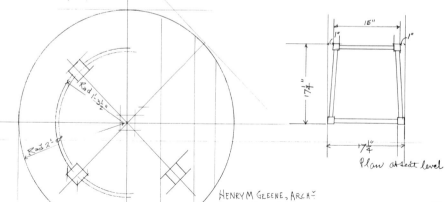

HENRY M GREENE, ARCH~
DINING TABLE & CHAIRS
Scale 1 IN = 1 FT

Plan at seat level

Above left:
Andirons, Henry M. Greene house, Pasadena, 1904. Marvin Rand photograph.

Above right:
Table designed by Henry for unknown client, circa, 1907.
Photograph courtesy Greene and Greene Library.

The design has characteristics similar to furniture for Mrs. Belle Barlow Bush.

Sketch by Henry Greene of dining room furniture intended for his own home.
Drawing courtesy Greene and Greene Library.

Tile inlay detail over den fireplace, Annie Blacker house, 1912. R. L. Makinson photograph.

Living room window, Annie Blacker house.

Henry's design for the living room windows breaks from the rigid linearity of the dining case glass, although the playful variations are almost mathematical in their progression.

Skylight in upper hall, William W. Spinks house, Pasadena, 1909. Marvin Rand photograph.

The linear geometrical design was typical of Henry Greene's compositions and here evolved from the natural expression of the structural framework.

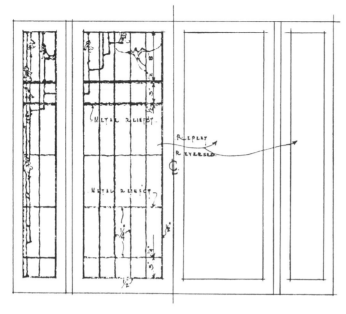

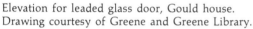

Elevation for leaded glass door, Gould house.
Drawing courtesy of Greene and Greene Library.

Even the nervous line of the leading in the drawing exhibits Henry's desire to soften and bring a more lyrical character into this leaded glass pattern accented by the free forms of birds in flight. Designs such as this exhibit the sensitivity and breadth of Henry's talents.

Wall lighting fixture for John Whitworth, Altadena, 1918. Marvin Rand photograph.

Combined here are forms from typical Greene fixtures of the wooden bungalow era with details and variations characteristic of the then popular Spanish Colonial Revival.

Below:
Wrought iron railing, Kate A. Kelley house, Los Angeles, 1924. Marvin Rand photograph.

In the 1920s Henry was able to pursue many of his interests in interior and furniture design. One of the first of these was in 1924 for the residence for Mr. and Mrs. Thomas Gould, Jr. for whom he designed an interior mirror for the landing of the stairwell, and clear leaded glass for the china cabinet where he was able to blend the lyrical movement of birds in flight with the regimented linear composition of the window. Soon afterwards the leaded glass for the windows for Mrs. Kate A. Kelly in Hollywood moved further from the straight line toward a more free and lyrical composition.

In spite of the long association between Mrs. Prentiss and Charles Greene, it was Henry whom she commissioned in 1925 for the designs for various pieces of bedroom furniture: a chair, a chaise lounge, a rocking chair for a drawing

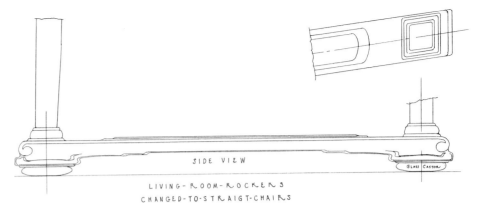

SIDE VIEW   GLASS CASTOR

LIVING-ROOM-ROCKERS
CHANGED-TO-STRAIGT-CHAIRS

Henry's concept to convert the living room rocking chairs designed for the Culbertson sisters to straight chairs for Mrs. Prentiss, 1925.

The sensitivity of the shaping of the wood stretcher of this design and the draftsmanship of this drawing by Henry are testimony of his multifaceted talents.

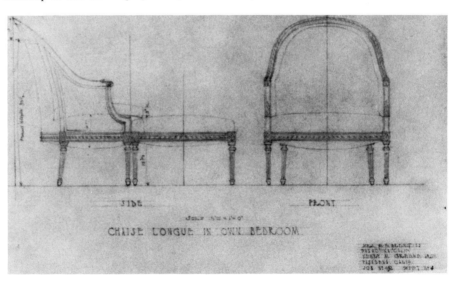

SIDE   FRONT

CHAISE LONGUE IN OWN BEDROOM

Sketch of proposed bedroom chaise lounge for Mrs. Francis F. Prentiss, 1925. Drawing courtesy Avery Architectural Library.

Tradition returns in the style of this chair; yet Henry has drawn the spirit of the wood detailing from the earlier furniture in the house designed by Charles.

Left:
Stained glass window, Kate A. Kelley house, Los Angeles, 1924.
Marvin Rand photograph.

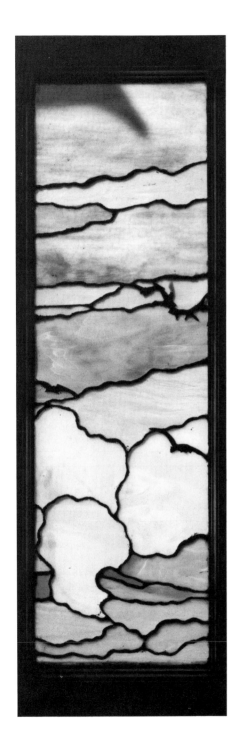

143

room, and designs to change the living room rockers to straight chairs. I assume that these rockers had been part of Charles' earlier designs, although there is no documentation for this assumption. While the details for the bedroom chair and the chaise lounge seemed inspired by historical furniture styles, the designs for the rocking chair for the drawing room bridged the traditional style with the furniture which Charles had designed earlier for Mrs. Prentiss. Henry's studies for converting the living room rockers to straight chairs clearly indicated his ability to handle the sensitive scale and movement of lines so often

identified solely with Charles Greene's designs. The drawing for the new base of the rocker was so sensitively proportioned, and the curvature of the line and the forming of the wood so gracefully handled that it might have come from the hands of Charles, although the quality of the drawing, the pencil work, and the lettering identify it definitely as the work of Henry Greene.

Another project was the design of an executive office for the Pacific Southwest Trust and Savings Bank in Pasadena in 1926. Apparently Henry was engaged to develop the office, complete with the wall paneling, furniture, and car-

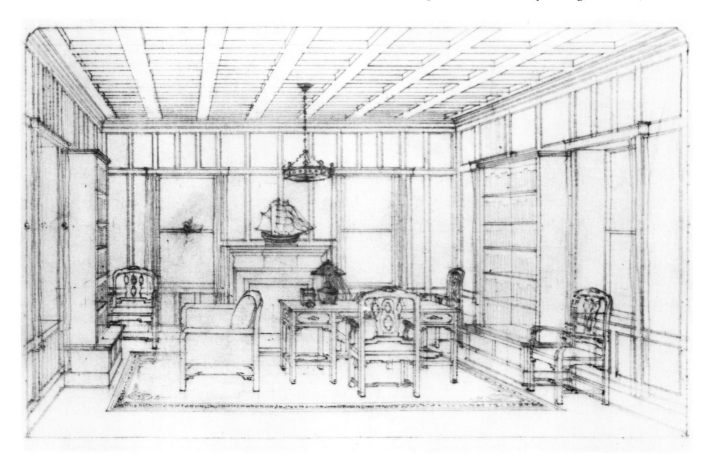

Sketch for project for an executive office, Pacific Southwest Trust and Savings Bank, Pasadena, 1926.
Drawing courtesy Avery Architectural Library.

Henry's furniture here appears related to designs for the elaborate bungalows of 1907-1911, to Charles' proposals for the D. L. James furniture, while also being influenced by oriental chair designs.

peting. This is the only indication that Henry was ever involved with carpet design. The furniture, however, was the most elaborate of Henry's designs. It departed from his normal linear austerity and became quite sculptural, much more like the furniture which Charles was designing for the ultimate bungalows between 1907 and 1910. There was an Oriental flavor to the desk, the chairs and the couch. Again, several schemes were carried no further than initial sketches, and apparently this too never went beyond the drawing boards. What is important, however, is the evidence of Henry's ability to adapt to differing situations and in so doing to handle his designs with a sensitivity for scale, proportion and line.

Following his second moving of the Jennie A. Reeve house (1904) in Long Beach, Dr. V. Ray Townsend turned again to Henry Greene in 1927 to resite the structure and fully develop the gardens including walks, fencing, gates and lighting. Townsend was so devoted to the design of the house that he commissioned further pieces of furniture which Henry designed to relate to and be used with the original furniture which was still in the house. Though there were differences in detail and subtleties of form representative of years of refinement and experience, Henry's new pieces had a contemporary quality which drew from the basic straightforward character more typical of the brothers' earliest furniture designs.

Small table for Dr. V. Ray Townsend, 1927.

One of several tables designed to complement Dr. Townsend's furniture which had been made for the Jennie A. Reeve house in 1904.

Living room table for Dr. V. Ray Townsend, 1927.
Marvin Rand photographs.

145

In 1929 Henry received one of his last and most important commissions, a residence in Porterville for Walter L. Richardson, to be built of adobe blocks made by the men on the ranch from materials from the soil. Here his concerns involved not only the design of the building, but the hardware (which was forged right on the site by the ranch hands) as well as some portions of the lighting fixtures. Most significant was the design of a walnut dining table in 1930. The purity of line and scale of proportion makes it one of the finest pieces of furniture ever designed by either of the brothers. If Henry Greene had designed no other

Detail of door knocker and hinges wrought and hammered by the ranch hands from Henry's designs, 1929. Marvin Rand photograph.

piece of furniture than this, the Richardson dining table would be ample testimony to the creative talent which he brought to the design of furniture. Its structure is direct, it is softened by recognizable characteristics identifying it with earlier works of the firm, it is light in scale, and reaches to the future. Structurally inventive, Henry composed a system of drop-leaves at each end which when not in use folded under and were kept in place by the notch in the end of the stretchers used to support the leaves when lifted into place to extend each end of the table.

> Henry Greene gets credit for some straightforward solutions to table extension problems in the dining table from the Richardson house. Leaves folding beneath the table, out of the way, are no innovation, but two details deserve attention. His supporting sliders do double duty as notched holders for the tucked-under leaves. The ganged hinges are oriented to reveal only the round barrel when the leaf is folded under. The hinge barrels would obstruct the action of the sliders, unless one cleverly formed the sliders to drop down slightly to clear the hinge barrel as they pull out, then come up to provide support. A short notch cut in the top of the slider provides clearance during the last inch or so of its extension, when it comes up to full supporting level.[2]

When folded under, the rectangular flush wooden pegs which were a part of the wooden joinery were sufficient decoration in themselves. Beyond the simple, straightforward fastenings of the structure there is no applied decoration. The purity of scale, line, and the grain of the wood are sufficient.

It is ironic that about the same time that Henry was designing such a progressive piece of furniture he would write to Charles that he was concerned with the coldness and lack of beauty that he saw in the machine-made products of the modern age.[3] While he was a wood craftsman at heart, his sense of order and direct response to situations made him, more than Charles, an architect on the eve of the Modern Movement.

2. Marks, Alan. "Greene and Greene: A Study in Functional Design," *Fine Woodworking*, (September, 1978) p. 43-44.

3. Correspondence between Henry Greene and Charles' wife Alice, courtesy of Robert Judson Clark.

Dining table for the Walter L. Richardson house, 1930.
Marvin Rand photograph.

The engineering for the folding end leaves of this table
exhibits an inventive spirit which is only matched by the
simple elegance of the extraordinarily progressive design.

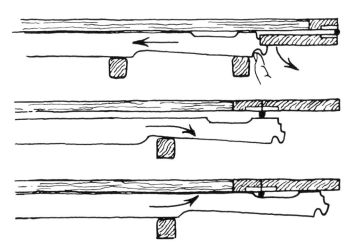

Detail of folded leaf of Richardson dining table.
Marvin Rand photograph.

Left:
Illustrations showing engineering concept behind folded
table leaf construction and support.
Drawing by Alan Marks, Courtesy *Fine Woodworking* magazine.

The close association that Charles and Henry had for many years might tend to make it difficult for many to determine the component parts of their combined efforts. Throughout the years, whether the work dealt with the architecture, interiors, furniture, or related designs, mutual respect and high regard made possible the production of some of the finest examples of the Arts and Crafts Movement in America. Apart from the architecture produced by the firm of Greene and Greene, there is little question that Charles Greene's genius created furniture and related designs which clearly represent high achievements of the Arts and Crafts Movement in the United States. At the same time, the product of that imagination would not have been possible in the quantity, quality and craftsmanship were it not for the close association and invaluable support of his brother Henry, the master craftsmen John and Peter Hall, Emil Lange, and the many fine artisans who worked so closely with Greene and Greene.

Wall lighting fixture for Richardson ranch house, 1929.
Marvin Rand photograph.

Entry door interior detail and
hardware, Walter L. Richardson
house, Porterville, 1929.
Marvin Rand photograph.

In typical fashion Henry utilized
the brusqueness of the plank and
bolted construction to advantage—
giving an appropriate rugged
character and proper scale to blend
with the bold adobe and stone
structure of the ranchhouse.

EPILOG

I think C. Sumner Greene's work beautiful; among the
best there is in this country. Like [Frank] Lloyd Wright the
spell of Japan is on him, he feels the beauty and makes
magic out of the horizontal line, but there is in his work
more tenderness, more subtlety, more self effacement than
in Wright's work. It is more refined and has more repose.
Perhaps it loses in strength, perhaps it is California that
speaks rather than Illinois, anyway as work it is, so far as
the interiors go, more sympathetic to me....

He [C. Sumner Greene] took us to his workshops where
they were making, without exception, the best and most
characteristic furniture I have seen in this country. There
were beautiful cabinets and chairs of walnut and lignumvitae, exquisite dowling and pegging, and in all a supreme
feeling for the material, quite up to the best of our English
craftsmanship, Spooner, the Barnslys, Lutyens, Lethaby.
I have not felt so at home in any workshop on this side
of the Atlantic—(but we have forgotten the Atlantic, here
it is the Pacific!). Here things were really alive—and the
"Arts and Crafts" that all the others were screaming and
hustling about, are here actually being produced by a
young architect, this quiet, dreamy, nervous, tenacious
little man, fighting single-handed until recently against
tremendous odds.[4]

Charles Robert Ashbee — 1909
Chipping Campden, England

4. Excerpt courtesy Professor Robert W. Winter.

C. Sumner Greene and Henry Mather Greene photographed
on the rocky coastline below Carmel, circa 1950.
Cole Weston photograph.

Selected Bibliography

Caldwell, John Wallace. "A Graphic and Historical Inquiry into the Furniture of Charles and Henry Greene." M. A. Thesis, Department of Fine Arts, Los Angeles State College of Applied Arts and Sciences, Los Angeles, 1964.

Clark, Robert Judson (ed.) *The Arts and Crafts Movement in America 1876-1916.* Princeton: Princeton University Press, 1972.

Current, William R. and Karen. *Greene and Greene: Architects in the Residential Style.* Fort Worth: Amon Carter Museum, 1974.

(Greene, Charles Sumner). "Cordelia Culbertson Residence." *Pacific Coast Architect,* (March, 1914) pp. 10-11.

Hanks, David A. "The Arts and Crafts Movement in America, 1876-1916." *Antiques,* Vol. CIV, No. 2, August 1973, p. 225.

Kazor, Virginia Ernst (ed.) *Greene and Greene: The Architecture and Related Designs of Charles Sumner Greene and Henry Mather Greene: 1894-1934.* Los Angeles: Los Angeles Municipal Arts Department and University of Southern California, 1977.

Makinson, Randell L. "Greene and Greene," Chapter III; McCoy, Esther, *Five California Architects.* New York: Reinhold, 1960.

_____. "Greene and Greene: The Gamble House," *The Prairie School Review,* (Fourth Quarter, 1968), pp. 4-26.

_____. "Special Report—Greene and Greene," with photography by Yasahiro Ishimoto. Osaka: Kakenaka Komutin Co., Ltd., *Approach,* (Spring, 1975), pp. 10-29, ff.

_____. *Greene and Greene: Architecture As A Fine Art.* Salt Lake City: Peregrine Smith Inc., 1977.

Marks, Alan. "Greene and Greene: A Study in Functional Design." *Fine Woodworking.* (September, 1978) No. 12, pp. 40-45.

Roper, James H. "Greene & Greene," with photography by Marvin Rand. Little Rock: Bracy House, *American Preservation,* (April-May 1978), pp. 42-60.

Tracy, Berry B. (ed.) and Johnson, Marilynn. *19th Century America: Furniture And Other Decorative Arts,* New York: The Metroplitan Museum of Art, 1970.

White, C. H. "Teakwood for Interior Decoration," *Architect and Engineer,* (March, 1911), pp. 94-97.

Winter, Robert W. "American Sheaves from C.R.A." *Journal of the Society of Architectural Historians,* (December, 1971), pp. 317-322.

Index

Acknowledgements

In addition to those persons identified in the Preface, appreciation is extended to the following for their varying roles and contributions during the research for this book.

Eleanor Bush Allen
Richard and Wendy Anderson
Jerry Barclay
Mrs. B. E. Behrends
Beatrice Bush Bissell
Edward Blacker
Robert Blacker
George and Marilyn Brumder
Mr. and Mrs. John Caldwell
Leonard W. Collins
Marjorie Townsend Conley
William Cross

Harley and Jennie Culbert
Philip DeBolske
Donald and Marie Duffy
Paul Duffy
Flavia Flavin Edgren
Mrs. Guy L. Embree
Phillip J. Enquist
Mr. and Mrs. Conrad Escalante
Mr. and Mrs. George E. Farrand
Roy Flamm
Martin Flavin
Sean Flavin
Mrs. Mortimer Fleishhacker
Mortimer Fleishhacker, Jr.
Arthur Froelich
Fuller Theological Seminary
Mr. and Mrs. David G. Gamble

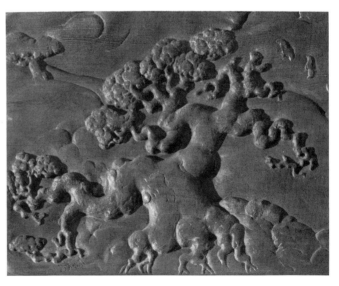

Mr. and Mrs. Edwin C. Gamble
Mrs. Sidney D. Gamble
Sidney D. Gamble
Constantine Gertmenian
Mrs. Penelope P. Gilde
Hank Gilpin
Mr. and Mrs. Douglas Goodan
Thomas Gould, Jr.
Isabelle Greene
Mr. and Mrs. Phillip Greene
Mr. and Mrs. Gary Hall
Nadine Hall
Dr. Robert Heebner
Max and Margery Hill
Mrs. Alice Hall Hodgkins
Huntington Library
Mr. and Mrs. Henry Hutchins

Dr. Hart and Patricia Isaacs
Mrs. Laura Ware Isham
Daniel and Lilith James
Mrs. John Bentz Jeffers
Eugene and Virginia Ernst Kazor
Rozene Kerry Lawrence
Mr. and Mrs. Robert Liefeldt
Richard Liu
Whitland Locke
Dr. C. Burke and Patricia Maino
Marie Marcus
James and Janeen Marrin
Margaret Meriwether
Elizabeth Gamble Messler
Dr. and Mrs. Joseph D. Messler
Kinzie and Irene Miller
Steven H. Milleron

Mrs. Mary C. Moore
Mr. and Mrs. Hartati Murdaya
Janice Nissen
Pacific Oaks College
Dr. Robert and Ruth Peck
Mr. and Mrs. David Pendell
Penny Penha
Mrs. Howard W. Porter
Daniel and Dorothy Power
Edvin and Margene Remund
James and Cynthia Richardson
William B. and Marjorie Richardson
Raoul and Patricia Savoie
Mary Gamble Sherr, Jr.
Julius Shulman
Sigma Phi Fraternity, Alpha Chapter
Scott Sinclair

Carleton and Betty Solloway
Mr. and Mrs. Frank Springer
Dr. Francis F. Spreitzer
Harlan and Margaret Gamble Swift
Philip and Rea Taylor
J. Eric and Elsa Thorsen
Mr. and Mrs. Arch Tuthill
Mr. and Mrs. Walter J. van Rossem
Karl W. Vancil
Dr. Robert Wark
Meg Wemple
Alexander and Edna Whittle
Mr. and Mrs. Harold Whittle
Mr. and Mrs. Orland Wilcox
Claus Willenberg
Richard H. and Elizabeth Townsend Winckler
Walter and Marilyn Hodgkins (Hall) Zaiss

Designed and produced by David L. Tilton
of Emmet L. Wemple and Associates,
Landscape Architects, Los Angeles
with the assistance of Laurie Burruss.